AF196061

Christopher Yusufu Mtaku

Continuity and Change

Center for World Music – Studies in Music

herausgegeben von
Raimund Vogels und Michael Fuhr

Band 5

Christopher Yusufu Mtaku

Continuity and Change

The Significance of the Tsinza (Xylophone)
among the Bura of northeast Nigeria

UV | O

Universitätsverlag Hildesheim | Georg Olms Verlag
Hildesheim | Hildesheim · Zürich · New York

2020

Christopher Yusufu Mtaku

Continuity and Change
The Significance of the Tsinza (Xylophone)
among the Bura of northeast Nigeria

UV | Q

Universitätsverlag Hildesheim | Georg Olms Verlag
Hildesheim | Hildesheim · Zürich · New York

2020

Diese Publikation entstand in Zusammenarbeit von Georg Olms Verlag und Universitätsverlag der Stiftung Universität Hildesheim.

Sie wurde vom Fachbereich 2 Kulturwissenschaften und Ästhetische Kommunikation der Universität Hildesheim zur Erlangung des Grades eines Doktors der Philosophie (Dr. phil.) als Dissertation angenommen.

Das Werk ist urheberrechtlich geschützt. Jede Verwertung außerhalb der engen Grenzen des Urheberrechtsgesetzes ist ohne Zustimmung des Verlages unzulässig. Das gilt insbesondere für Vervielfältigungen, Übersetzungen, Mikroverfilmungen und die Einspeicherung und Verarbeitung in elektronischen Systemen.

Die Deutsche Nationalbibliothek verzeichnet diese Publikation in der Deutschen Nationalbibliografie; detaillierte bibliografische Daten sind im Internet über http://dnb.d-nb.de abrufbar.

ISO 9706
Gedruckt auf säurefreiem, alterungsbeständigem Papier
Satz und Layout: Jan Jäger
Umschlaggestaltung: Inga Günther, Hildesheim
Herstellung: Docupoint GmbH, 39179 Barleben
Printed in Germany
© Georg Olms Verlag AG, Hildesheim 2020
www.olms.de
© Universitätsverlag Hildesheim, Hildesheim 2020
www.uni-hildesheim.de/bibliothek/universitaetsverlag/
Alle Rechte vorbehalten
ISSN 2367-4547
ISBN 978-3-487-15532-6

Dedication

To the memories of Magira Yahiniya

&

Yusufu Mtaku Midala

Acknowledgements

This work has been made possible thanks to the support and encouragement I received from some organizations and many people that I would hesitate to mention because they are so many. But I must thank my main supervisor, Prof. Dr. Raimund Vogels, whose scholarly criticism and advise has made this thesis possible. I am also grateful to Prof. Dr. Julio Mendívil for the time he has devoted to going through a great deal of ethnomusicology literature together with me and who has also contributed in the supervision of my project; making many suggestions that have shaped this work. Similarly, Prof. Dr. Thomas Hilder and Prof. Dr. Carl Florian have assisted in one way or the other. I am most grateful to all.

This work also has been possible by a grant from the German Academic Exchange Service (DAAD) at the start of my fieldwork some years back as well as a grant received from the Volkswagen Foundation for the funding of the joint research project, "Formation and Transformation of Musical Archives in West African Societies". I am most grateful for the support from both organizations. I must also acknowledge my employer, the University of Maiduguri/Nigeria, for the numerous leaves of absence granted to me to pursue my doctoral degree. The Center for World Music and the University of Hildesheim/Germany, have granted me a very conducive atmosphere for work at various times throughout my work on this thesis. I am most grateful for that.

I would also like to express my appreciation to all my teachers in the field; and the numerous people I interviewed in the course of the fieldwork for this thesis. Without sharing their knowledge of Bura culture with me, this work would have been impossible. Many were extremely patient with me and assisted in various ways to link me up with other people whom they knew could add to the knowledge they shared with me. I am most grateful to all.

My appreciation also goes to my dear wife and our two lovely children for their support and encouragement. They endured my absence from home, especially my several visits to Germany to work on the thesis. My wife especially had to cope with caring for the kids alone. I appreciate your sacrifices very much. To my brothers, sisters and in-laws, I say thank you for your encouragement and support and for always standing by my family while I am away.

Last, but not least, I would like to thank Kerstin Klenke for organizing some of my trips and stays in Hildesheim. Nadine Grobeis and Markus Korda have also been very helpful. I am grateful to Steve Oguabuaja, Habib Mohammed, and Harrison Idahosa for the illustration of musical instruments used in this thesis. I appreciate you all.

Table of Contents

1	**Introduction**	**15**
	1.1 Methodological Approach of the Study	18
	1.2 Outline of the Thesis	19
2	**The Relationship Between Past and Present**	**21**
	2.1 Introduction	21
	2.2 The Theories	21
	2.3 Conclusion	38
3	**The Regional Context and Environment**	**43**
	3.1 Introduction	43
	3.2 The Area of Study	44
	3.3 Traditions of Origin and Migration	46
	3.4 Occupation	49
	3.5 Political Organization.	49
	3.6 Worldview and Religion.	50
	3.7 The Colonialization of the Bura	51
	3.8 The Bura as Subject of Anthropological and Linguistic Research	56
	3.9 Conclusion	57
4	**The Bura *Tsinza* Xylophone**	**59**
	4.1 Introduction	59
	4.2 The Tsinza in the Context of Other African Xylophones	60
	4.3 Tsinza – Oral History	66
	4.4 Construction of the Tsinza – A Case Study	70
	4.4.1 Construction and its Language	77
	4.4.2 Decoration and its Meaning	79
	4.4.3 Organological Description of the *Tsinza*	82
	4.4.4 Regional Differences in Construction and Decoration	83
	4.4 Conclusion	85

5   A Linguistic Approach to the Description of Bura Musical Instruments   **87**

5.1   Introduction   87
5.2   Drums and their Ways of Beating – Sur tsayeri na fit fitari
       ka kisim (Membranophones)   88

       5.2.1 Ganga   88
       5.2.2 *Kwala*   89
       5.2.3 Words Describing or Naming Musical Ensembles
              with only Drum Instruments   92
       5.2.4 Words Describing or Naming Musical Ensembles
              with Drum Instruments and any Other Instrument   95
       5.2.5 Words Describing or Naming Musical Ensembles
              with Drum Instruments and Singing   95
       5.2.6 Words Describing or Naming Musical Ensembles
              with Singing Only   97

5.3   Suryeri ar Mbura ka Mya (Aerophones)   100

       5.3.1 Shola   100
       5.3.2 *Algaita*   100
       5.3.3 Timbul   102
       5.3.4 Hyika   102
       5.3.5 Words Describing or Naming Musical Ensembles
              With Aerophones   103
       5.3.6 Words Describing or Naming Musical Ensembles
              with Aerophones and any Other Musical Instrument   104

5.4.   Sur Tsayeri ka Nvada na Kula Fita (Idiophones)   104

       5.4.1 Bara   104
       5.4.2 Kace – Kace   105
       5.4.3 Humbutu   105
       5.4.4 *Kugwa*   107

5.5   Sur Tsayeri na ka Mpila Fit Fita ka Suwur Puwa
       (Chordophones)   107

       5.5.1 Gulum   108
       5.5.2 Yakandi   109

5.6   Conclusion   109

6   The *Tsinza* in its Traditional Context   111

     6.1   Introduction   111
     6.2   Bura Funerals   115

           6.2.1   Funeral Rites of an Adult Bura Man   116
           6.2.2   Funeral Rites of an Adult Bura Woman   122
           6.2.3   Funeral Rites of a Young Bura   124
           6.2.4   Funeral Rites of a Chief   125
           6.2.5   Funeral Rites of Blacksmiths   126

     6.3   Repertoire of Bura Funerals—A Case Study   126
     6.4   Tsinza as a Medium of Communication   136
     6.5   Conclusion   141

7   The Introduction of Christianity to Bura Land   143

     7.1   Introduction   143
     7.2   The Beginning of Mission Work   143
     7.3   Impact of the Missionaries on Bura Land   146
     7.4   Conclusion   150

8   The *Tsinza* in its Contemporary Context   153

     8.1   Introduction   153
     8.2   Bura Occasions of Musical Activities   153

           8.2.1   *Bansuwe* Dance   157
           8.2.2   *Kildzi/Lausa* (Wedding)   157
           8.2.3   Christian Occasions   159
           8.2.4   Christian Funerals   161

     8.3   Conclusion   166

9   Summary and Conclusions   169

Bibliography   179

List of Figures and Maps

Fig. 1. Klaus Wachsmann's Scheme of Investigation for
         Ethnomusicology. (Wachsmann 1971: 96)   28
Fig. 2. Present and types of history in ethnomusicology (Bielawski
         1985: 11)   33
Fig. 3. Jauro Msirawa carving a sound plate with *nkum mara*   71
Fig. 4. Tools for *Tsinza* Construction (*nkum mara, indla deaha* and
         indla)   72
Fig. 5. Kugwa *Tsinza*   74
Fig. 6. Setting of resonators in the Kugwa tsinza   75
Fig. 7. *Tsinza* Player   76
Fig. 8. *Tsinza* Players   79
Fig. 9. *Tsinza* Decoration   80
Fig. 10. *Tsinza* Decoration   80
Fig. 11. *Tsinza* Organology   82
Fig. 12. *Ganga*   89
Fig. 13. *Kwala*   90
Fig. 14. Dlimbwal   91
Fig. 15. *Shola* player   101
Fig. 16. *Algaita*   101
Fig. 17. *Timbul* player   102
Fig. 18. *Hyika*   103
Fig. 19. *Bara*   104
Fig. 20. Kace–Kace Players   105
Fig. 21. *Humbutu*   106
Fig. 22. Alhassan Saltuwa and group performing *Humbutu* music. 106
Fig. 23. *Kugwa* players   107
Fig. 24. *Gulum* player   108
Fig. 25. *Yakandi*   109
Fig. 26. Schematic diagram of Hertz's arguments (Metcalf and
         Huntington 1991: 83)   112
Fig. 27. Scheme of Communication in the Bura Story of Origin of
         Death   139
Fig. 28. Scheme of Communication through *Tsinza* at Bura Funerals 140
Fig. 29. Decoration type of some of the tsinza used in Christian
         context   160
Map 1.   Map of Nigeria showing Bura land shaded grey in the
         northeast.   43
Map 2.   Map of Borno State Showing Biu Plateau in the South   44

1   Introduction

This thesis concerns the Bura xylophone, *tsinza*. It focuses on its roles amongst the Bura people who live in the southernmost part of Borno State and the northern part of Adamawa State in northeast Nigeria. The *tsinza* occupies a special position in Bura culture. It is closely linked with Bura identity. Old musicians emphasize that it was originally an important funeral instrument. Today, however, the instrument has assumed other roles with an entirely different meaning for many. Drawing from the current roles of the instrument, my thesis will explore why and in what ways the Bura maintain *tsinza* music/performance, even though the traditional context of the music is disappearing.

I am a Bura man. Growing[1] up as a child in Bura land up until the present, *tsinza* music has always captured my interest. As a child though, I was never allowed to go close to where this music was performed. However, children are allowed to stand some distance away to observe what is going on if the music is being performed in the daytime. If it is at night, children are not allowed outside the house, but the music of the instrument can be heard all around the village.[2] Back then, the meaning of the mainly instrumental music was hard for me to understand. Questions pertaining to the meaning were never directly answered fully by the adults around. The answer had always been, "you are too young to understand now, and you will know the meaning as you grow up".

One particular Sunday, I was surprised to hear the *tsinza* being used as accompaniment to church songs. I can recollect that on Sundays, I was not at the church service,[3] but in my father's compound located just about 20 meters from the village church. I could hear everything going on in the service without being in attendance. I remember running out of the compound to the church to confirm whether it was actually the *tsinza* that was being played. At that time, we were used to the sound of the accordion, which was brought by the American missionaries and used as an accompaniment for the Bura hymns translated from the hymnbook they brought. This time, the sound I heard sounded different from the accordion. Upon reaching the church, I saw what I thought I had heard; my guess was correct. It was actually the *tsinza* being used in the church. From that period on, I witnessed the instrument being used more and more at Christian funerals, weddings and other Bura social events as I grew up in the village.

---

1   I spent my formative years as a child and teenager in the village of Garkida.
2   Garkida village was very small at that time.
3   It was considered mandatory to attend church services.

Later in life I understood why I, as a child, had to keep some distance from the instrument and why my questions regarding the music of the instrument were never directly answered. Many of the adults around then, including my parents, had some time ago converted to Christianity.[4] As in many other parts of the world where missions were started, the first demand by the missionaries that came to Bura land was that converts denounce many of their indigenous beliefs and cultural practices.

The Church of the Brethren Mission (CBM) was the first in America to open a mission field on Bura land in 1923, with a Mission Station based at Garkida. It is a Christian denomination with origins in the Schwarzenau Brethren that was organized in 1708 by Alexander Mark in Schwarzenau, Germany. The United States church was established in 1723. The denomination holds the New Testament of the Bible as its guidebook for living. It holds it as the record of the life, ministry, teaching, death, and resurrection of Jesus Christ, and of the beginnings of the life and thought of the Christian church. Its distinctive practices include believer's baptism by trine immersion: a threefold love feast consisting of washing of the feet, a fellowship meal and communion, an anointing for healing, and a holy kiss.

Based on the distinctive practices of the Church, the missionaries condemned outright what they saw of the practices of the Bura traditional society and set up new requirements for entering into the new Christian fold. The *tsinza* tradition was one among many of the practices considered to be 'evil' by the missionaries. Therefore, the Bura converts should not have been seen associated with the instrument.

The missionaries' teachings that some of the people's practices were "evil," had a significant impact on the role of the *tsinza* amongst the Bura people. However, it did not stop completely their use of this instrument. Many Bura did not convert to Christianity. Even those who did convert were still required by tradition to attend all funerals of the members of their clans,[5] and to attend other Bura social events where *tsinza* music is performed.

Being a Bura man myself, the instrument and its music continued to be of interest to me though a lot of questions remained unanswered. It was not until I worked with Prof. Dr. Raimund Vogels, a German ethnomusicologist, as a research partner on a Project titled, the 'Borno Music Documentation Project,' (B.M.D.P.) from 1989 to 1990, that I became more inquisitive about the *tsinza*. The purpose of the project was to document traditional music in Borno State. Among the documented music of the many ethnic groups that reside in Borno State is that of the Bura. The *tsinza* featured prominently in the documentation of Bura music. In the course of the documentation work, many of the questions I had as a child regarding the instrument and

---

4 Christianity made inroads into Bura land in 1923.
5 Bura social organization is largely based on clan relationships.

its music resurfaced again. I gathered that the role of the instrument has changed over time and has acquired different meanings for many Bura people. This triggered my interest to undertake a study of how the *tsinza*, originally said to be an important funeral instrument, is adapting to changing social conditions within Bura society. How the musical practices in the context of religious ritual experience been transformed over the course of the period of the encounter of the Bura people with the missionaries, and, how indigenous religious practices and imported religions have influenced each other with regard to musical culture in a historical perspective, are the key questions that I seek to address in this thesis.

Many of the Bura abandoned the *tsinza* at a time of general confusion of dealing with the intrusion and adoption of the new religion, new medicine and new culture that came with the missionaries. Many of the converts at the beginning of the missionary work were young people. The missionaries, however, encountered resistance to the new way of life by the older generations at the beginning of their missionary work to "modernize" the Bura because of the pressure exerted on them, for example, to let go of their funerary practices, and some of their wives[6] in order to only retain one in accordance with the Christian creed seeing marriage as constituted by "one man, one woman", and so on. Perhaps, the most impactful thing for the Bura during that period was the demand to let go of their funerary practices in which the *tsinza*, that is said to be closely associated with their identity, played a major role.

Today, many indigenous musical practices of many African societies are fast disappearing. However, the *tsinza* music tradition certainly does not count among those traditions. Despite the general impact of the activities of the American missionaries on the indigenous culture of the Bura, the *tsinza* music tradition is still today a lively art amongst the people. While it was true that many of the Bura Christian converts at the beginning of mission work in the area abandoned the *tsinza* tradition, which to some extent led to the reduction of those that partake in it, the situation is quite different today.

Soon after the church of the Brethren in Nigeria became independent from the church of the Brethren in America in 1973, the *tsinza* made inroads into many of the churches[7] found in the area; though it is used in an entirely different context in the church. It is used as accompaniment to church hymns at all important Christian ceremonies within and outside the church, e.g. marriage, funeral and so on. What is interesting is that many

---

6   Many Bura people were married to more than one wife at the time the missionaries arrived in the area.

7   The church established by the American missionaries remains the dominant church denomination in the area to date. Other denominations have, however, started in the area not to long ago.

young people[8] are now the players of the *tsinza,* both at church services and at Christian wedding receptions, funerals and so on. Also interesting is that the tunes performed at the wedding receptions are not church tunes but rather praises of the groom, bridegroom, their relations and those who patronize the musicians.

While many older *tsinza* players are of the view that some of the songs performed by the younger musicians at wedding ceremonies in particular, are funeral songs the younger ones seem to have a different interpretation of their music. They are quick to point out that the tunes they perform are those that their patrons enjoy, and as a result, from which they attract monetary gains for singing their praises. Many of the younger *tsinza* musicians being Christians, they do not now associate anything "evil" with the instrument as portrayed by the early American missionaries. Perhaps, the perception of the instrument as not being "evil" is what has kept the *tsinza* tradition a living art amongst the Bura people as it to some extent still plays important roles within the society despite the changing social conditions.

The adoption of Christianity by some of the Bura certainly brought about a change in how they perceive the music of the *tsinza.* It can be said that a change occurred not only within the context in which the instrument is used, but also in the musical systems. For example, the use of the instrument in church services creates new contexts in which it is used as well as a new musical style, which differs from the traditional one. While in the traditional context the music played for a funeral is purely instrumental, at church services, and, indeed at many other Bura social events, it is accompanied by singing through call-and-response. This is a clear indication of a significant change both in the context of use of the instrument and its musical system. It is the change in context of the use and musical system of the *tsinza,* mainly brought about by the adoption of a new religion, i.e. Christianity, which is the central theme of this thesis.

1.1 Methodological Approach of the Study

The main method employed in undertaking this work is qualitative ethnographic research. I mainly draw on techniques derived from social anthropology and ethnomusicology, most importantly participant observation as well as semi-structured interviews with *tsinza* musical specialists, religious groups and churches, as well as knowledgeable people within Bura society. Historical methods have also been utilized in this study. I have consulted references by early scholars and accounts of early travelers, explorers and

---

8   The older generation of players seem to have largely remained adherents of Bura traditional religion.

missionaries.[9] As a strategy to study the religious change that led to the *tsinza* tradition being abandoned by many Bura at the beginning of the area's period of Christianization, and its later reacceptance – to the extent that the instrument has assumed many roles in the society, including being used in churches – I draw to some extent on the role it played before in the area the introduction of Christianity. Older *tsinza* musicians insist that the instrument was purely a funeral instrument. As a result of this insistence, and in order to have a better understanding of its current role in Bura Society, I explored to some extent, the *tsinza* in its traditional context. I also draw from the formative years I spent growing up around the missionaries, as well as what my parents and grandparents told me later in life concerning the instrument, and my current experiences of the role it plays amongst the Bura people. I relied more on oral sources due to the non-existence of written sources on Bura music. Also, I adopted the strategy of taking back to the field what ever I wrote from my field notes to the few Bura elites – mostly retired schoolteachers – for discussion. Many of them reside in the area and are also *tsinza* players with some knowledge about the instrument themselves.

As an insider of the Bura culture though, I am not unmindful of the issues related to the debate on the emic and etic perspectives in anthropological, social and behavioral sciences (Geertz, 1975, 1983, Gregory, 1993, Goodenough, 1970, Headland & Harris, 1990). It is possible that in the course of fieldwork for this thesis, I may not have noticed things that are obvious because they form part and parcel of my everyday life and I interpret them accordingly. Nonetheless, my main goal is to study the *tsinza* and analyze it from a scholar's point of view. In this regard, in my discussion of the *tsinza*, not only did I rely on the information that I gathered through fieldwork, but I also framed the study in relation to theories and approaches used by other scholars in other studies done on reconstructing music history.

1.2 Outline of the Thesis

This thesis is divided into nine chapters. Chapter 1 introduces why I chose this topic and the issues under focus in this study. In Chapter 2, the focus is on theories that discuss the nature of the "past" and "present" and the role of memory in the reconstruction of cultural history. I put forward and summarize theories by numerous scholars and point out how some of these theories are relevant to this work. In Chapter 3, the regional context and environment of the study area is discussed with an emphasis on the Bura complex – its people, geography, language, political organization, worldview, and the colonialization of the area. The Bura xylophone is the focus of

---

9   Some of the missionaries that worked in Bura land trained as anthropologists.

Chapter 4. Its oral history, construction, organology, and relation to other African instruments, i.e. other xylophones with a similar order of keys, are also discussed in this chapter. Linguistic approaches to the description of Bura musical instruments and the different ways of playing them are discussed in Chapter 5. This chapter also considers Bura terminologies that relate to music, which are also used in every day language to refer to other things or situations. This is done with the aim of determining some aspects of the people's worldview that might be embedded in the language used in discussing music generally. Chapter 6 discusses the *tsinza* in its traditional context, i.e. as a funeral instrument. For a better understanding of the importance of the *tsinza* in Bura funerals, a detailed description of the funerals of the various categories of Bura people, such as adult male and female, young person, chief, blacksmith and those killed by lightening, are given in the chapter. I have done this in order to determine what the people consider as their "funeral rite". It is unclear from the little available literature what role the *tsinza* plays in Bura funerals. The funeral of a *tsinza* master musician is used as a case study to further understand the traditional repertoire of Bura funerals.

During the course of fieldwork for this study, I was able to observe the construction of the *tsinza,* and to participate in both traditional and Christian funerals. Such occasions provided me the opportunity not only to observe, but also to have in-depth discussions with many elderly Bura people. The cases observed in the field constitute some of the aspects that are discussed in Chapters 4 and 6 of this thesis.

Chapter 7 on the other hand, will focus on the introduction of Christianity to Bura land. The adoption of Christianity constitutes the "immediate past history" of the Bura (Bielawski 1985: 10). Emphasis is placed on the effect of the activities of the missionaries that settled in the area on Bura indigenous culture, especially the *tsinza* xylophone tradition. The role of the *tsinza* in contemporary Bura society is the focus of discussion in Chapter 8. This chaper investigates how the use of the instrument is negotiated in contemporary Bura occasions for musical performance, for example in official, ritual, and private contexts. The instrument has assumed roles other than that for which it is originally said to be, i.e. funerals. That being so, some elements of the "past" are in the "present," but the context of use and the meaning of the instrument differs between the older and younger generations. Chapter 9 is a summary of the entire work and also contains concluding remarks on the study.

2 The Relationship Between Past and Present

2.1 Introduction

The past as it pertains to music is a subject that has been taken on by many ethnomusicologists in the discourses on music change. Many of these scholars, apart from discussing the issue of methodology, have in particular theorized the nature of the "past" and "present," and the role of memory in reconstructing music history. Such theories focus on the interdependent nature of the past and the present. As demonstrated by some of the theories, the present will always contain elements of the past. Correspondingly, memories of the past are constantly changing and influenced by new events that occur in society everyday. This chapter summarizes some of the theories developed by ethnomusicologists that focus on the importance of the relationship between the past and the present in the reconstruction of music history. This is done with the aim of identifying those aspects that are useful for the theoretical frame of this work. I shall follow a chronological order, beginning with the work of Bruno Nettl, followed by other authors according to the year of publication of their work.

2.2 The Theories

Bruno Nettl presents a selection of what he terms, "the most influential and most promising theories and studies," in ethnomusicology in a chapter of his book, *Theory and Method in Ethnomusicology* (Nettl 1964: 224). He discusses the historical and geographic approaches to the study of music in culture. He observes:

> "It seems to be the most convenient to divide the study of music in culture into two broad areas: the study of the individual group, or person, or nation in one place and at one time; and the study of music in its spatial (i.e., geographic) and temporal (i.e., historical) environment. The first of these areas would seem to be a prerequisite to the second, but as is so often the case in a young discipline, the broader and more difficult questions have been broached before the narrower and perhaps less obviously fascinating ones. Thus there is much more theory and method available on the study of change of music, and on the geographic distribution of music, than there is on the study of music's role in one culture or in one person's life. Studying the geographic distribution of musical phenomena and the ways in which music changes, and participates

in culture change, is more important to an understanding of the role of music in culture" (Nettl 1964: 225).

Nettl explains that the historical aspects of ethnomusicology "can be grouped into two principal classes – origin and change" (Nettl 1964: 226). However, at the early stages of the discipline of ethnomusicology the focus had been placed on the origin rather than on change, the later being of greater interest if the problems of methodology were resolved. "Change" and "origin" as problems are often related and combined, but both require different approaches when it comes to studying them. Nettl discusses the number of ways that these problems can be approached. According to him, in approaching origin as a problem, "one may be interested in the manner of origin of a given phenomenon, or its place of origin" (Nettl 1964: 226). However, the manner of approach in the study of "origin" in ethnomusicology has been one of the more speculative aspects of the discipline, even though "ethnomusicological data can only corroborate or, more frequently, negate" (Nettl 1964: 226). The search for the manner of origin of various generalized musical phenomena and, the treatment of specialized or localized phenomena are also possible approaches to origin.

The problem of "change" according to Nettl, requires a different approach, as most often ethnomusicologist are interested in the reasons for change or lack of change, its nature, degree, and rate (Nettl 1964: 227). He observes that

> "[w]e can study the change in individual compositions or in larger bodies of music. We can try to trace the changes indicated by differences among the variants of single song, and we can try to identify the reasons for them, whether these lie within the structure of the music or its cultural context. We can try to measure, for comparative purposes, the amount of change that has taken place and try to determine how rapidly it has occurred. Similar matters can be studied-but with greater difficulty in entire repertories, whether defined geographically or by their cultural milieus" (Nettl 1964: 228).

The focus of this thesis is on change in the cultural context within which the *tsinza* is used. The observation by Nettl of identifying the reasons for change, whether they lie within the structure of the music or its cultural context is therefore useful. Thus, attention is paid to the reasons for the change in the cultural context within which the *tsinza* is used.

Nettl also describes "geographic movement" as an important factor to consider when studying change. He notes:

> "[...] investigations involving change are frequently associated with those concerning the place of origin of a musical phenomenon, for the obvious rea-

son that if a musical item moves from one place to another, it is also subject to change, and it would be impossible to assess the change without considering the geographic movement" (Nettl 1964: 228).

My investigation of change in the context within which the *tsinza* is used does not involve geographic movement of any sort. The instrument rather has been part and parcel of Bura culture as long as the people can remember.[10] The only kind of movement associated with it, is its having been said to be an important funeral instrument to its being used by the Bura at many other social events today. Nettl's suggestion of considering geographic movement would therefore not be used in assessing the change in the cultural context of the use of the *tsinza*.

One of Nettl's suggestions of two ways of studying individual cases of historical change in "folk and non-literate" cultures and their music is, however, useful for this thesis. He notes:

"There are two ways of studying individual cases of historical change in folk and non-literate cultures and their music. One can try to reconstruct events of the past, or one can observe the changes occurring at the time at hand" (Nettl 1964: 237).

In this thesis, I reconstruct the funeral rites of the Bura, where the music of the *tsinza* is said to have been an important component accompanying all the various stages of the rites. This reconstruction will not only provide an understanding of the changes that have occurred in the cultural context within which the instrument is used, but also allow for a comparison with the past.

In a similar vein to Nettl, Alan P. Merriam (1967) discusses the use of music as a technique of reconstructing cultural history in Africa. He identified three different approaches in which music can be used to achieve this: (i) description of a way of life of a people at a given point; (ii) culture change; and (iii) using specific tools, which describe what is unique or special about it. He pointed out, however, that the potential importance of music to this kind of problem might vary widely because of its special characteristics (Merriam 1967: 86). For example, he notes:

"So far as it is known, no African culture ever independently developed a notational system for its organization of culturally-defined musical sound; this means there is relatively little hope of reconstructing the aural shape of African music with any accuracy ... some attempts have been made along this line, either through special archaeological techniques or through the application

---

10   Only through oral history can we find out about the *tsinza* since literature on Bura music is generally very limited.

of a priori anthropological theory, but such attempts do not seem particularly effective or reliable" (Merriam 1967: 86).

However, Merriam also notes:

"[...] music is represented not only by sound but by musical instruments as well, and some of these instruments have survived over considerable span of time. Thus, in dealing with music as tool for historic reconstruction, we must consider the music and the instruments and be prepared to use either or both as the possibilities present themselves" (Merriam 1967: 86).

With regard to the first approach, he considered three general categories within which it can be done: through song texts, use of music and musical instruments, and reconstruction through archeology. As for song texts, his idea is that at any particular time it contains certain information about a people. Such information can be used in reconstructing cultural history by linking it to historic accounts about a people's way of life. This, according to him, is especially true in the case of Africa, which seems to be of limited time depth. However, for the reason of his argument in the quotes above, the first approach of tracing of the actual sound of music to any substantial time depth cannot be a very effective or reliable method of reconstructing cultural history. The problem of the "authenticity" of texts in terms of the accuracy of message or description conveyed could also be an issue with this approach. The approach is, therefore, not important for this thesis and it shall not be followed. To the best of my knowledge the songs played on the *tsinza* appear not to contain any historical narrations. Rather, they are funeral songs that seem to deal with the issue of mourning and may not necessarily contain any historical narration other than praising the achievements of a deceased person while alive. However, attention would be given to a comparison of praise[11] in the past and what obtains in present times.

As for reconstructing cultural history through music and musical instruments, Merriam explains that music is not only represented by sound, but also by musical instruments. Therefore, musical instruments can be very valuable in reconstructing cultural history through the analysis of change in the instrument itself, change in the context within which it is used, and change in the music that people make with it. Some instruments have survived over a considerable period of time and in such cases could be used for analysis. Thus, for example, references by early scholars and accounts of early travelers, explorers and missionaries could give remarkable information that can be used to provide comparison to determine whether an

---

11   Musicians of the instrument sing the praise songs of their patrons for monetary rewards in recent times as well.

instrument, or the context within which it is used, has undergone changes over a period of time. I find this approach useful and important for this thesis on the Bura *tsinza*.

My interest lies mainly in looking into the change in the context within which the instrument is used. The 'change in context' I am interested in could be looked into by reconstructing the use of the instrument in indigenous funerals rites and comparing it with its uses in today's Bura society. To the best of my knowledge, there seems to be cultural continuity in the musical forms of the *tsinza,* but the context within which it is used appears to have significantly changed. As my focus is on the context in which the instrument is used, rather than on musical forms, I will not engage in analysis of the music of the tsinza.

The field of archeology provides the third in Merriam's set of methods through which cultural history can be reconstructed. Archeology can be used to ascertain a description of cultures and their use of music at any given point in time, as Merriam discussed. Musical instruments can be compared to archeological findings. Whilst this may be possible in arid regions of Africa, as in the case of Egypt, it is more challenging in many areas where most musical instruments are made of wood and the environment is not arid enough to preserve the instrument (Merriam 1967: 91). The *tsinza* is made of wood[12] and to the best of my knowledge there is no record of it being preserved and forming part of any archaeological record. There is unfortunately no way of comparing it with any archeological artefacts.

Another major approach to the reconstruction of cultural history discussed by Merriam, "involves the possibility of using music to establish the theories of grand processes which operate throughout time" (Merriam 1967: 93). He discussed some of these theories pointing out that they can be used in the reconstruction of cultural history, though their use may be problematic. According to him:

> "The possibilities of using evolutionary schemes in reconstructing culture history are [sic] not particularly bright. In order to do so, we must make assumptions, which do not seem tenable; for example, if one finds the stick-and-membrane bellows in one location, and friction drum in another, it must follow, according Balfour, that culture of the first people is older than that of the second. Similarly, the culture of people who use the simple hunting bow must be older than that of people who use instruments of several strings. Or people who use two- or three-note melodies have older cultures than those who use six- or seven-note melodies" (Merriam 1967: 95)

---

12   It is made of wood as well as other materials from the natural environment e.g. bee wax, spider, cattle horns etc.

The logic of such propositions, according to Merriam, can be followed without difficulty, but the problem, however, of such theories is that they are based on speculations. "Logic and deductive theory", according to him, "are not substitutes for empiricism" (Merriam 1967: 95). He explains that evolutionary theories of the development of music based on the comparison of an array of facts from cultures around the world have their own problems. He notes:

"Least acceptable today are evolutionary theories of development of music, particularly those which, through the use of what is now regarded as an invalid comparative method, array facts from cultures around the world into systems which "prove" a deductively formulated theory" (Merriam 1967: 93).

Such comparison, according to him, lead to "formulations - which have devised systems of cultural stages through which mankind is said inevitably to move" (Merriam 1967: 93). Thus, the basic assumption in all evolutionary schemes is that culture develops chronologically from the simple to complex; an assumption that is always very difficult to verify and to work with.

Merriam also asserts that the same kind of criticism can be applied to *Kulturkreis* (cultural circle) theories. Such theories, as demonstrated especially by the speculation of Friedrich Ratzel on the similarities between West African and Melanesian bows, which was later taken further by Leo Frobenius' (1898) and George Montandon's (1919) culture circles, and Sachs' (1929) and Hornbostel's (1933) theories, are also based on assumptions of "layers of time" (Merriam 1967: 100). Such speculations are also difficult to prove and to work with, especially now that factual information that was not available during the time of these scholars exists. Referring to the *Kulturkreis* theories formulated by some of these scholars, Merriam notes:

"How useful are theoretical formulations such as theses? There seems, first of all, little reason for accepting the propositions forwarded by Frobenius and Montandon [two leading exponents of culture circle]. This is partly because factual information is now available which did not exist some sixty years ago and which makes certain of their assumptions untenable, but mostly because both appear to have been dealing with a priori schemes for which they were intent upon supplying facts. The severest criticism must be directed toward assumptions of "layers of time" (Merriam 1967: 100).

He explains that such theories can also be used in the reconstruction of cultural history, but with some limitations. He emphasized that it is especially possible if the diffusion framework of "culture cluster," as proposed by Sachs (1929) and Hornbostel (1933), is used. He writes however that:

"... one is struck by the extra ordinary range of knowledge of music instruments brought to the theories; and it seems clear that the results might may well be reasonably accurate in the broadest perspective. Logic is on their side, and in this case, logic is carefully buttressed by fact; the major difficulty, again, is in accepting the three premises regarding the diffusionary process; and if we cannot accept them on the scale proposed by Sachs, then the theory must fall. The approaches taken by Hornbostel and Sachs appear more reasonable than those advanced by Frobenius and Montandon because they represent a step in the direction of greater control of materials within the framework of diffusion studies" (Merriam 1967: 100, 101).

Merriam is thus of the view that comparative approaches within a closed area can be useful. The concept of culture cluster, according to him, "seems to be a valid concept much more precise than the older area concept in handling distribution of culture traits and the movements of peoples" (Merriam 1967: 103). For example, the *tsinza* can be compared with the xylophones of the Tera and Ga'anda, both ethnic[13] groups neighbouring the Bura. Thus, by implication, using the diffusion approach in such a comparison is more useful than comparing the *tsinza* with xylophones in Asia. The xylophones found in both ethnic groups have the same order of keys, but are played in a different way. Music, according to Merriam, "is a creative aspect of culture, which through recording, can be frozen as it happens... and can be repeated over and over and studied in detail" (Merriam 1967: 108). Its structure can be transcribed on paper and expressed precisely through arithmetic and statistical means (Merriam 1967: 108). I am not comparing the musical forms of the *tsinza* with those of the neighbouring groups with similar instrument in this thesis. Therefore, Merriam's second approach to reconstructing cultural history is not useful to this thesis.

The third approached discussed by Merriam is the study of either music pitch or music structure to reconstruct cultural history. It is possible to make precise comparisons between music styles. If a music style can be expressed with precision and, if it does have an individual integrity, the technique can be used for the reconstruction of cultural history. The problems with this approach though are the question of sampling (i.e. music pitch or music structure) and of deciding which elements of the music style are significant. Again, this approach is not important for this thesis considering the fact that it is not looking into *tsinza* music styles.

Unlike Nettl and Merriam, Klaus Wachsmann (1971) presents a diagrammatic scheme through which music historians can systematically carry out an historical investigation into music. He presented the lines of attack tra-

---

13   Northeast Nigeria comprises of over 200 ethnic groups and it is a zone of intensive interaction among the groups.

ditionally represented by music historians (vertical arrows I – IV) against the various levels of historical investigation that scholars of African music ought to work with (horizontal rectangles A – E).

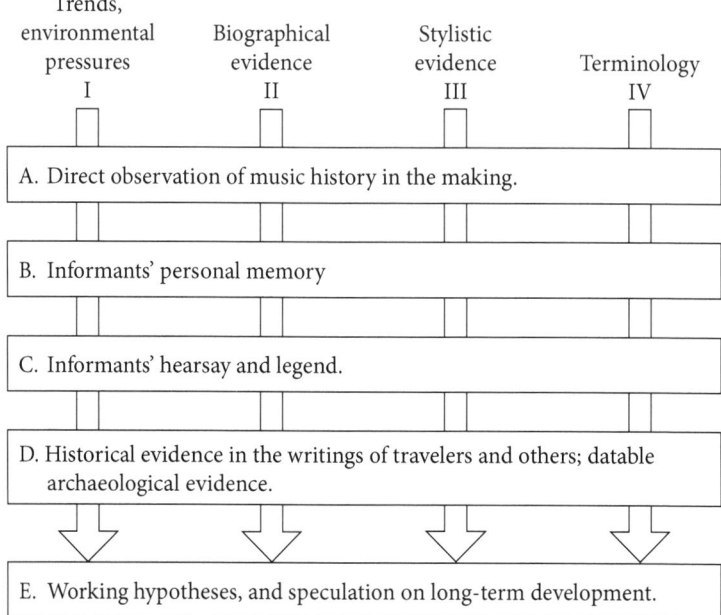

Fig. 1.   Klaus Wachsmann's Scheme of Investigation for Ethnomusicology.
(Wachsmann 1971: 96)

Wachsmann explains his scheme thus:

"Music historians, given opportunity and experience, ought to feel thoroughly at home with level A at all its intersections with the four arrows. It is here that their contributions will naturally be at its best. At level B much will depend on the informant's awareness of musical sound and his ability to put his knowledge into words. In oral tradition, in Africa as anywhere else, this is notoriously difficult, and it becomes progressively more so as one moves to level C and D; especially at their intersection with arrow III, the quest for information will mostly be in vain. Consequently, any data found along arrow IV that may have survived in speech are likely to remain musically meaningless. At level E music historians may take refuge in the assumption that oral tradition can be extremely stable, so stable indeed that experience at level A might make it legitimate for them to speculate on and to construct working hypotheses with regard to the earlier stages of any musical culture" (Wachsmann 1971: 95).

Wachsmann's scheme of historical investigation is central to this thesis. It is the scheme that is mainly adopted, but consideration has been given to the other theories discussed in this chapter. However, Wachsmann's procedure, as in his own case of studying musical instruments in the Kiganda tradition, would be reversed in the presentation of my data on the investigation of the *tsinza*. Instead of starting from level A, I would start with a long-distance view of the instrument reaching the present with the hope that a clearer picture of change in context would emerge in this chosen manner of presentation.

In his work on some problems of theory and method in the study of musical change, John Blacking (1977) discusses some problems inherent in the theoretical perspectives developed by the traditionalist (or "purists") and the modernists (or "syncretists") - as he termed those that developed them. He observes that

"[t]he traditionalist... have neglected the dead weight of traditional routines, as the modernists... have seemed unaware of the superficiality of merely fashionable changes, and both have failed to distinguish the varieties of musical change and the level at which they operate, or relate them to other changes that are taking place in the society, especially changing relationships between classes and changing patterns in the allocation of power. It can, in fact, be argued that all evaluations of musical change tells more about the class and interests of the evaluators than about the real nature of musical change" (Blacking 1977: 3)

Furthermore, he also observes that:

"Studies of musical change should focus on change that is specifically musical, and change that really is change. The kinds of music that are made are an obvious focus of musicological interest, but they are the products of processes in the behaviour of the species and the action of groups and individuals" (Blacking 1977: 6).

The focus of this thesis is not to investigate change in *tsinza* music structure per se. However, the adoption of Christianity by many of the Bura changed their perception of the *tsinza* and its music. While it was true that the American missionaries did not condone the use of the instrument in the church, through the churches' view "that music itself must be spiritual in order to be suitable for things eternal" (Wachsmann 1958: 55), the Bura found a new context within which the *tsinza* could be used by bringing it to the church after it was handed over to the indigenous people in 1973.[14] The instrument

---

14   The period when the American missionaries handed over the control of the church to the Bura people.

is no longer considered "evil" by the people inasmuch as it is used in Christian religious contexts. The attitude of the Bura who have adopted Christianity as a new religion has brought about significant changes to the context within which the *tsinza* is used. It has made it possible for the music to be adapted to other Bura social events other than the traditional context with which it was associated (funerals).

Blacking's theory that "all musical change must be considered from both synchronic and diachronic perspectives, and always in their social context" (Blacking 1977: 19) is very useful for this thesis. The adoption of Christianity by some of the Bura people could be said to mark the beginning of observable change with regard to the *tsinza* and its music. Christianity as a new social institution among the Bura brought about a change in the conceptualization of the instrument and its music. Playing the instrument in the church and at other Christian related activities are, for example, new contexts that have created new musical orientations amongst many in the society. While the techniques of playing the instrument remain the same, it is now adapted to entirely new repertory that fits the new contexts within which it is performed. The instrument remains the same from an organological point of view, but its sociocultural function now differs in today's Bura society.

Mantle Hood (1982) also discusses the "historical past" as an important source of reconstruction of musical culture in ethnomusicology. He observes that:

"Almost any subject of research in music, even in the most contemporary, can be related in some manner to the historical past. And the sources of history are virtually unlimited. Annals, chronicles, literature, artifacts, monuments, bas-reliefs, sculpture, painting, illuminated manuscripts, the technology of agriculture, of metal work, of pottery, of architecture, and so forth, together furnish the historian with the bits and pieces of evidence that constitutes the factual skeleton of his narrative reconstruction. Through induction, inferences, and imagination he attempts to recreate the probable past" (Hood 1982: 337).

Hood notes, however, that such diverse types of evidence produce correspondingly diverse reconstructions among historians to the extent that the ethnomusicologist, in an attempt to understand the cultural history of a given society, may find himself or herself "caught up in the finical debate of the scholarly arena" (Hood 1982: 337). The diverse types of evidence and reconstructions may be difficult to evaluate by the ethnomusicologist since "they are subject to a patent chauvinism" (Hood 1982: 337). Few facts and an "excess" of inferences are mostly the outcome of such reconstruction to the extent that it is difficult to say with "certainty what relates to music in its socio-cultural milieu" (Hood 1982: 338). However, Hood notes that:

"Exposure to the vagaries of differing histories is in itself, enlightening. But it is to the sources of history relating to music that the ethnomusicologist must turn. Interpretation of these particular bits and pieces of evidence fall clearly in his sphere of expertise, and such an enterprise not only may furnish helpful clues to the historian but also may contribute to the research objectives of the ethnomusicologist" (Hood 1982: 338).

Hood also explains that special attention deserves to be given to "a particular kind of historical source not uncommon in ethnomusicological research" (Hood 1982: 338). By this he refers to certain types of music practice in Asia, whose historical past has remained unbroken, according to him. He observes that:

"In many musical cultures of Asia, ancient types of musical ensembles are still in usage, so that the historical past of music, to some degree, has managed an unbroken continuity to the present. The extent to which the musical style and instrumentation of such and may have changed through the centuries is, of course, a question that must be posed. But the viability of such ensembles is usually ensured through their association with religious and/or secular ritual which itself is highly resistant to change. Often, therefore, the ethnomusicologist has the good fortune to be able to work in the here and now within a kind of living laboratory of the historical past of music" (Hood 1982: 338-339).

Hood's assertion that certain "religious" and/or "secular" rituals are highly "resistant" to change cannot be generalized. The *tsinza*—although not an Asian instrument—is said to have been an instrument associated with death rituals and did not resist change. However, his point of "working in the here and now within a kind of living laboratory of the historical past of music" is useful for this thesis. Of course, the present use of the instrument is quite significant in reconstructing its historical past. This point will be therefore explored.

Hood also explores "comparison" and "criticism" as an important method in historical reconstruction. According to him:

"Comparative and critical methods are continually involved in the course of description, analysis, synthesis, and the processes of historical reconstruction. The habit of comparison and the exercise of critical judgment tend to become an almost automatic response to certain kinds of research problems. And, of course, either comparison or criticism may become an end in itself" (Hood 1964: 342).

He, however, disagrees that comparative musicology is the principal aim of ethnomusicology. Rather, "comparative studies at various levels of concentration can be identified among the important objectives of the ethnomusicologist, when sufficient knowledge of the musical cultures being compared is at hand" (Hood 1964: 342). He explains that the "levels of concentration" that might have special significance need to be taken into account when comparing musical cultures. He notes:

> "If a study centers on the Compositional Devices of The Composer or the Improvisational Devices of The Performer [sic], for example, it is likely to have greater significance if it includes comparison with the practices of other contemporary composers or Performers in The Tradition [sic]. The implications are even greater if it extends to include comparison in historical depth. In the same way, the study of a collection of Pieces or a Genre will be enhanced if it includes comparison with other kinds of pieces or genres within the Tradition [sic]" (Hood 1964: 343).

This thesis is not centered on a comparison of the sort given as an example by Hood. However, the aspect of "time depth" is significant for this work. A reconstruction of the context within which the instrument is used would be important in understanding the "change in context" that has occurred in its use among the Bura people.

Like the other works discussed above, Ludwik Bielawski (1985) discusses the subject of history in ethnomusicology. He observes:

> "Investigations into any music require two supplementary and interdependent orders: the systematic order (of quality and quantity) and the historical order in time and space (contact and continuity). This basic truth has not always been realized" (Bielawski 1985: 8)

He speaks of a concept of history in ethnomusicology, which gives special attention to the "present" time. According to him:

> "Any review of the types of history in ethnomusicology should give special attention to the present time, as history must always relate to the present. The later determines the perspective of historical processes, as it is in the present that views of the past are formed" (Bielawski 1985: 10).

He suggests that historical problems can roughly be divided into five major sections, namely: 1. the immediate history of local societies, 2. the mythical past and tradition, 3. the complete history of a given culture or group of cultures, 4. the history of mankind and stages in the evolution of the world's musical cultures, and 5. the musical aspects in anthropogenesis (Bielawski 1985: 10). He presents the historical problems in a diagrammatic form:

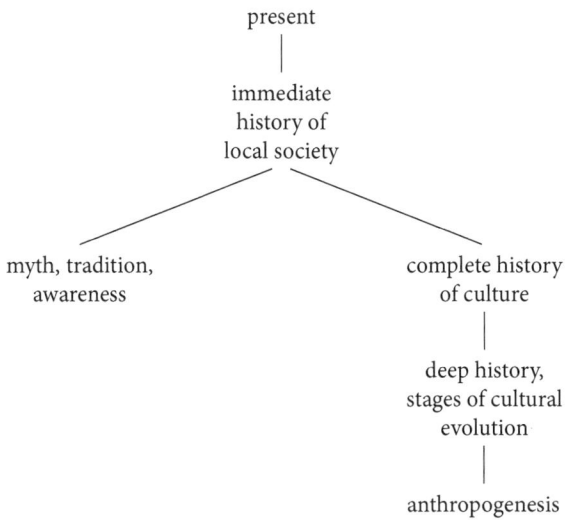

present

|

immediate
history of
local society

myth, tradition,   complete history
awareness   of culture

|

deep history,
stages of cultural
evolution

|

anthropogenesis

Fig. 2.   Present and types of history in ethnomusicology (Bielawski 1985: 11)

Bielawski further notes that:

> "Immediate history, held in the memory of living generations, must be regard-
> ed as particularly important in ethnomusicology since it can be a common
> denominator for historical investigations into all existing musical cultures,
> no matter how complex they are and whether or not there are documents to
> support them. The immediate history of local societies varies [sic] throughout
> the world. It may constitute the first insight into the past and is directly con-
> tiguous with the present" (Bielawski 1985: 10).

This concept further provides a useful perspective for this thesis. The "colonialization" and, particularly "missionization" of most parts of Bura land,[15]
constitutes part of its people's immediate past history. This "immediate
past history", going by Bielawski's concept, could be applied to studying the
changes that occurred in the indigenous practices of the Bura people, especially with regard to that of the *tsinza* tradition.

In an introduction to a selection of case studies on the theme "Past in
Music", Caroline Bithell (2006) on the other hand, shares her thoughts on
the nature of the past and the role of memory in reconstructing historical narratives with reference to the way in which these concepts have been
theorized by historians, archaeologists, anthropologists and ethnomusicol-

---

15   Bura land first came into contact with the colonialist in the 19th century.

ogists. Her concept is that music retains the past, and the present cannot be understood without reference to the past. She observes:

> "It may well be a truism to say that there's no escaping the past. 'Whether it is celebrated or rejected, attended to or ignored, the past is omnipresent' (Lowenthal 1985, xv). Not only is it all around us, in the contours of our landscapes and the fabric of our cities. It is in our blood; no matter how we try to erase or forget it, it insinuates itself into our dreams" (Bithell 2006: 4).

The present therefore, has a history. The present cannot be interpreted without "appreciation of the historical dimension" (Bithell 2006: 3). For "it is the meaning invested in assumed memories of the past that gives present actions their rationale. The present may be unimaginable without the past, but it is the present that calls the shots" (Bithell 2006: 5). She discusses models proposed by a number of writers for "distinguishing different levels of past-ness". These include: a ritual noncontested past, a precapitalist agricultural past, and a 'modern' past (Bithell 2006: 5). The model of a 'ritual non-contested past' is especially very useful for my work. In line with Bithell's notions of the past, a reconstruction of the traditional Bura funeral would shed light on the present context within which the tsinza is used.

Bithell also discusses Assman's (1992) identification of two modes of remembering the past – "communicative memory" and "cultural memory". The earlier "refers to the recent, more concrete past", while the later "refers to the distant past, with ritual playing a primary role in its organization" (Bithell 2006: 6). This thesis largely looks into the 'cultural memory' of the tsinza. Her explanations of this mode of remembering the past are also very useful for this thesis. Music, according to her, "can both reference the past and carry it forward in numerous ways" (Bithell 2006: 7). Different pasts can be brought together as well, and recontextualized in the present. Bithell observes that

> "[d]ifferent pasts and their meanings coexist. Part of the attraction of "the past" in our own age is that it presents us with "an infinity of alternative worlds" (Butt 2002, 171) onto which we can project a multitude of meanings and interpretations. We are free to choose the face of the past in which we recognize our own present or future" (Bithell 2006: 5)

In the case of the tsinza, it can be said that it has been taken from its traditional context of being a funeral instrument (past) and recontextualized into the church and other Bura social events (present). A major focus of this thesis is the application of differing opinions, interpretations, and meanings ascribed to the context of use of the tsinza.

Like Bithell, Kay Kaufman Shelemay (2006) also explores the relationship between music, memory and history during the ethnographic research process. She observes that there is a symbolic relationship between memory and history:

"Like oral history, musical ethnography provides an open window on the construction of historical narratives. ...Ethnomusicologist do not simply gather individual and collective verbal memories shared during interviews; they are also instrumental in elaborating memories in and about musical performance into narratives about the past. The ethnographer is thus an important but largely unacknowledged player in the elicitation of memories and the construction of histories" (Shelemay 2006: 18).

Drawing from data of interviews with Syrian Jews about a hymn *pizmon* repertory, she discusses the past in the present as conveyed through music. She suggests that

"[...] within shared social worlds – domains anthropologist have traditionally termed "cultures" or "subcultures – verbal and musical forms do not simply occupy the same times and spaces but can converge through the workings of memory in both their form and content" (Shelemay 2006: 20).

Also, she proposes that "within ethnographic interviews, expressions of memory are transformed by all participants to construct history" (Shelemay 2006: 20). Thus, according to her "intersections or "crossroads" of memory and history takes place within the exchanges about music and music-making that constitutes the ethnographic interview" (Shelemay 2006: 20). Using the data from the interview on *pizmon,* she discusses the dimensions through which the transformation of memory into historical narrative can be explored. These include: 1. "the interaction of individual and collective memories in the recollection of musical experience," 2. "memory processes, including the moments of encoding that may be understood as taking place during musical performance and reception," 3. "musical memories as intertwined with affect emotion and nostalgia," and 4. "patterns of repetition and reinvention so crucial within musical performances and memory processes alike" (Shelemay 2006: 21). The first relates to "storage spaces" as metaphors for memory. "Language relating to or describing memory", according to her, is "largely metaphorical" in almost all societies (Shelemay 2006: 22). Therefore, musical sound conceived as a "storehouse" for memory can be explored to construct history. The second relates to "moments of encoding that may subsequently cross into multiple domains." For example, "individual memories of hearing a song may be re-inscribed and reconstituted in forms ranging from dairies to sound recordings" (Shelemay 2006: 26). Mention of such written texts or recordings during ethnographic interviews or participant observations can cue memories that can be used in historical reconstruction. The third has to do with emotional memories. According to Shelemay, music carries many types of memories, which are directly implicated in three different memory systems: episodic memory, semantic memory and procedural memory – all considered being part of long-term memory (Shelemay 2006: 28). The domain of episodic memory especially, if fully explicated, can be very useful in the construction of music history. Episodic memory as Shelemay explains "permits the recall of specific incidents". Many important life-circle events and rituals, for example, are associated with music and such events, are, according to Shelemay, "replete with emotions that play a crucial role as music is encoded and recalled" (Shelemay 2006: 28). This is true as observed in the case of the performance of the *tsinza* at a wedding during the course of fieldwork for this thesis. An older[16] *tsinza* musician got emotional upon hearing one of the tunes (*Para*) being performed by a younger player. He recalled that it was a tune that was performed to "escort" a corpse to the grave, but was now being played at a wedding ceremony to entertain guests.

Lastly, the fourth aspect of Shelemay's theory on the creation of historical memory has to do with repetition. The "intentional re-composition of old tunes in new context" helps construct a history of transmission and, "repetition is important for processes of memory and historical continuity" (Shelemay 2006: 31). Shelemay's ideas in regards to the relationship between music, memory, and history provide a valuable perspective for this thesis. The reconstruction of the use of the *tsinza* in the traditional context is largely based on the data collected from interviews with informants. The idea of "intentional re-composition of old tunes in new context" will in particular be explored; as the *tsinza* is presently used in other contexts than that which the Bura said it was originally used for.

Shelemay and Bielawski's theories of reconstructing culture history through music appear to be similar to some extent. Both theories focus on the issue of "memory", "past," and the "present". The theories can also be looked at in the light of Wachsmann's (1971) scheme of historical investigation in ethnomusicology, one of the few exceptional theoretical models set for the study of music history that considers memory in its structure (see Fig. 2)

Both Shelemay and Bielawski stress the 'present' as a starting point for the various levels of historical investigation as suggested in Wachsmann's scheme. This is followed by the informants' memory of immediate past history, myths and legends, and historical records in the accounts of travelers, missionaries and others. Shelemay's theory, however, differs from those of Bielawski and Wachsmann, for their lack of the inclusion of what she termed as most important aspect of musical memory, "affect," in their schemes of investigation. By this she refers to the episodic memory discussed briefly above.

---

16   Old *tsinza* musicians seldom perform at wedding ceremonies.

This thesis follows the scheme of historical investigation for ethnomusicology as theorized by Wachsmann. As explained in the introduction to this
thesis, my interest in studying the *tsinza* was triggered by the encounters I
had as a child and later as an adult and field assistant[17] to an ethnomusicologist that documented the instrument in the late 1980s. Apart from being
a Bura man, I have observed directly the use of the instrument at many
occasions at various times, especially since I started studying it. Throughout the course of my fieldwork, I conducted several interviews in order to
document informants' personal memories of the instrument. Such personal memories of the informants include hearsay, legends, and myths about
the instrument. I also take into consideration the accounts of some scholars
who wrote on the xylophone in Africa. The data generated by these steps of
historical investigation is what is presented in this thesis. I give special attention to affect, to deal with what Shelemay observed as an important ommis-
sion from Wachsmann's scheme of historical investigation in ethnomusicology. Particular attention is given to the "episodic memory" of older *tsinza*
players especially when a younger player is performing at an occasion.

Using the Jewish music of Burgenland, Philip V. Bohlman explores in
a similar manner, "the boundary regions of the ethnomusicological past"
(Bohlman 2008:246). According to him, only when he returns to the ethnomusicological past does he "find comfort in the search for the meanings
of both the past and present in the Jewish music of Burgenland" (Bohlman
2008: 247). He observes that:

> "The emergence of fieldwork as a research method in the social sciences has
> resulted to a large degree from its capacity to bring the scholar into contact
> with the present. The fieldworker not only makes observations in the present,
> but the present provides diverse frameworks for the several narratives report-
> ed by the fieldworker, through field notes, accounts of participant-observa-
> tion, or full-blown ethnographies" (Bohlman 2008: 248).

Bohlman notes though that a "fieldworker's encounter with the present is an
uneasy paradox" (Bohlman 2008: 248). Fieldwork, according to him, is an
excursion into the culture of the "other" and must account for "everyday"
practices; with the "other" and "everyday" being at extreme opposite ends
(Bohlman 2008: 248). Similarly, "culture" and "practice" appears to be at
opposite ends as well. It is however, "temporal considerations that sharpen
the paradox" (Bohlman 1997: 248). Bohlman observes that:

---

17   I worked as field assistant to an ethnomusicologist at University of Maiduguri/
Nigeria between 1989 and 1991.

"Whereas the everyday and its practices would seem to unfold within the present, the culture of the Other [sic] requires a systematization, even ossification, of moments gone by. The present, therefore, is ongoing, but once inscribed in ethnography, it is marked by the syntax of pastness. The past, in contrast, is frozen in a timelessness, from which it must be wrenched to be synthesized into the presentness of history. The disjuncture between past and present makes it increasingly difficult for fieldwork to examine either, but necessary to examine both" (Bohlman 2008: 248).

It is clear from this passage that the "past" cannot be studied without taking the "present" into consideration and vice versa. It is nonetheless necessary to identify the "ethnographic and historical space" that fieldwork opens up. For it is such that serves as a "discursive space of boundaries, not boundaries between culture, instead a space within which cultures locate themselves" (Bohlman 1997: 248, 249). He notes:

"These boundary spaces undo many of the categories that ethnomusicologists and those involved in fieldwork have long taken for granted. Culture within these spaces no longer forms into systems, but rather become fluid, ephemeral, and contested. History can no longer be recuperated into teleological narratives that 'once happened' and can now be told again and again in their inscribed versions. History, too, forms in a temporal space, contested because fragments of the past remain in the everyday of the present" (Bohlman 1997: 249).

Again, from the above, Bohlman's argument is that there is no one ethnomusicological past, but many. It is therefore, the responsibility of the ethnomusicologist to explore those many pasts. The arguments presented by Bohlman are important for this thesis. The *tsinza* cannot be studied without taking both its "past" and "present" into consideration. The "many" pasts of the instrument will be explored as well as its "present". Culture as a non-homogeneous entity, but as a polyphonic reality will also be taken into consideration.

2.3 Conclusion

This chapter has brought together some of the literature that discusses theories and methods in ethnomusicology dealing with the study of musical change. All the authors discussed theorize the relationship between the "past" and the "present" and how its mutually dependent nature can be employed in reconstructing cultural history. They all argue that the echoes of the past can still be heard in the present (Bithell 2006) and there is no way a study of musical change or reconstructing culture history can be undertaken without considering both the past and the present. The texts considered in this chapter, therefore, allow me to question the relationship between the past and the present in the case of the context within which the *tsinza* is used. The studies suggest various ways in which such studies can be undertaken.

Nettl (1964) proposes two ways of studying individual cases of historical change in "folk and nonliterate cultures." The first way is by reconstructing events of the past and, the second by observing the changes occurring in the present. In either way, both are dependent on the other. Events of the past cannot be reconstructed without taking the present into consideration. Similarly, the present cannot be "observed" without recurring to the past. In both cases an appreciation of the dimension of involvement of each with the other is very important in reconstructing cultural history. Hood's (1964) ideas are similar to those of Nettl. He speaks about the ethnomusicologist having the good fortune of working in the here and now in musical practices considered to have "managed unbroken continuity" into the present. The existences of such practices are very doubtful though, since it could hardly be true to say with certainty that a musical practice has existed with unbroken continuity. To the best of my knowledge the tradition of the ritual instrument, *tsinza*, has been broken. Changes in musical style and instrumentation do occur to some extent in musical practices. In the case of the *tsinza* a change in the context of use seems to have occurred. Hood, however, suggests comparative and critical methods as processes that can be employed in the study of musical change or historical reconstruction. This suggestion is important in the case of the *tsinza*. A general question, though, that this study will consider, is how the past and the present context of use can be taken into consideration in reconstructing its cultural history.

In his discussion of the basic techniques that can be used for exploring Africa's past, Merriam (1967) focuses, too, on the relationship between the past and the present. His ideas though are more diverse than those of Nettl and Hood. Three key points characterize his ideas: (i) description of the culture of a people at a certain time, (ii) development through time (i.e. history as process of time), and (iii) anything unique or special about the tool (i.e. musical instrument) that makes it relevant to the problem of reconstructing cultural history. All these ideas would only have some meaning if the relationship between the past and the present were taken into consideration. Whether describing the way of life of a people, their development through time, or the cultural continuity of an instrument, the past and the present dimensions are relevant. There has been, for example, cultural continuity in some aspects of the *tsinza*. The technology of constructing the instrument and the manner of playing it has remained the same, but the context within which it is used has changed. To study such a change in the use of the instrument, therefore, both its past and present context of use need to be taken into consideration. The investigation into the change in the context of use is best approached through the instrument itself since it is part of the Bura culture, and culture moves through time (Merriam 1964: 92). Thus, the culture of the *tsinza* at a "certain time" can be described or compared, but such a description or comparison would always require its past or present dimensions to reconstruct its cultural history.[18]

Wachsmann's (1971) scheme of historical investigation for ethnomusicology (see Fig. 1) demonstrates clearly the relationship between the past and the present. His presentation of the lines of attack traditionally represented by music historians (vertical arrows I – IV) against the various levels of historical investigation that scholars of African music ought to work with (horizontal rectangles A – E) demonstrates this relationship. "A" as a starting point is a direct observation of music history in the making; this refers to the "present". "B", "C" and "D" deal with the informant's personal memory, hearsay and legend, historical evidence in the accounts of travelers, and archaeological evidence respectively, which could be seen as the "past". To apply the scheme, therefore, both the past and the present need to come into play. Wachsmann's scheme is the main theory that is adopted and applied to this investigation into the change in context of use in the *tsinza*. However, its application will be reversed in order in the presentation of my data; instead of starting my presentation with the present, the past of the instrument will be considered first. It is from the past context of use that its present will be considered in order to understand the changes that have occurred. I have observed the present and through doing so, I have noticed some elements of the past. By reconstructing the past first, the present can be understood.

To buttress Wachsmann's theory, the ideas of Bielawski (1985), Bithell (2006), Bohlman (2008) and Shelemay (2006) on the past and present are also taken into consideration. All of the authors discuss how music creates a connection between the past and the present, emphasizing the relationship of memory and history during the ethnographic research process. Their ideas are important for this work. Shelemay considers Wachsmann's scheme of historical investigation for ethnomusicology as one that incorporates memory on both his diachronic and synchronic axes, but does not include one of the most important aspects of musical memory – affect (Shelemay 2006: 27). As I use Wachsmann's scheme of historical investigation for this work, her observation is noted and incorporated.

In addition to the main theory selected for this work, Blacking's theory that "all musical change must be considered from both synchronic and diachronic perspectives, and always in their social context" (Blacking 1977: 19) is also very useful. The introduction of Christianity to Bura land marks the

---

18   In case of the *tsinza*, its having been said to be a funeral instrument constitutes its "past" and, the current uses, its "present".

beginning of a significant shift in the way of life of the people. The impact of Christianity on some of the indigenous practices of the people—particularly the *tsinza* tradition—is, thus, a big consideration. To what extent has Christianity as a new social institution among the Bura brought about a change in the context of use of the instrument, is one of the questions that this study will consider. How has playing the instrument in the church and at other Christian related activities created new contexts that have in turn created new musical orientations amongst many in society? Nowadays, as observed in the course of fieldwork for this thesis, the instrument is used at official, ritual, and private occasions. Such occasions include both Christian and Moslem[19] occasions. The society, however, remains predominantly Christian. So, the focus would be more on the influence of Christianity on Bura musical occasions. It is, therefore, the hypothesis of this thesis that the reconciliation and integration of Bura indigenous practices within a new religious system (i.e. Christianity) has created continuity and change in the role of the *tsinza* amongst the people. As a result, some aspects of the "past" are visible in many of the "present" contexts within which the instrument is used.

In the next two chapters, I shall examine the regional context and environment of the area of study, and the history and construction techniques of the *tsinza*, which are of central concern to this thesis. The later especially constitutes part of the "past history" (Bielawski 1985: 10) of the Bura people, and is of significant importance in my attempt to reconstruct it's "past" and "present" history.

---

19   Some of the Bura embraced Islam when it made in-roads into the area.

3 The Regional Context and Environment

3.1 Introduction

Northeastern Nigeria comprises six states[20] of Adamawa, Bauchi, Borno, Gombe, Taraba and Yobe. These six states cover an estimated area of 310,666 square kilometers. The area borders three countries: to the north is Niger Republic and to the east is Chad Republic, whilst the Republic of Cameroon lies to the east and southwest.

Map 1. Map of Nigeria showing Bura land shaded grey in the northeast.[21]

The most distinctive feature of the states of northeastern Nigeria is its diversity. Nigeria, as a whole, consists of over 250 ethnic groups and over 400 languages. Many of these ethnic groups live in the Northeast. The Kanuri

---

20 Nigeria is made up of 36 Federal States and a Federal Capital Territory.
21 The map was created by Ishaku Yahaya.

43

and the Pabir/Bura[22] are the main ethnic groups in Borno, the most north-easterly state in Nigeria, where there are also few Shuwa Arab ethnic groups to be found.

3.2 The Area of Study

Bura land lies in the northeastern part of Nigeria. It is situated in the south-ernmost part of Borno State. By Bura land, one means the area located on the Biu Plateau, where the majority of the Bura people are found, as well as the northern part of Adamawa State where a small number of the people live.

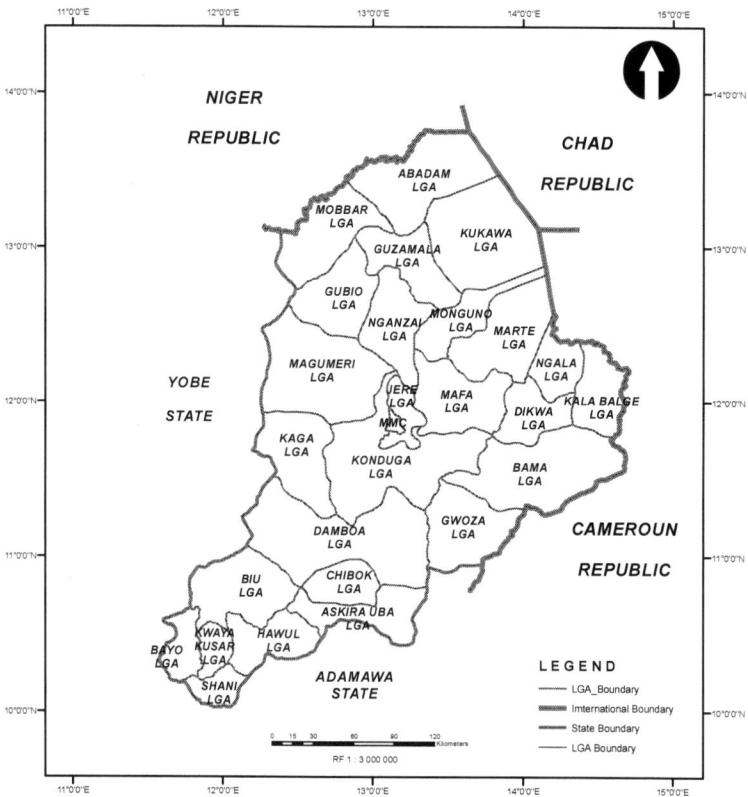

Map 2. Map of Borno State Showing Biu Plateau in the South[23]

---

22   The Bura speaking-peoples are divide into two groups. Those that live in Biu town and the area north of it, who are referred to as Pabir, while those that live south of the town are referred to as Bura.

23   The map was created by Ishaku Yahaya.

The Buras of Adamawa State are found in a village conglomerate, Garki-da, in the trans-Hawul Valley within the Gombi Local Government Area (LGA). Those who live in Borno State are found in four LGAs, namely: Biu, Hawul, Shani, and Kwaya Kusar. The area referred to as Bura land is divided into two regions, that of the Pabir Emirate of Biu in the North and Bura villages to the south. The dominant populations of the two areas speak a common (Chadic) language and practice many of the same beliefs and customs in terms of local economy, religion and other aspects of social life (Cohen 1988: 72).

Bura land has a tropical climate. The annual mean temperature is about 80°-85° Fahrenheit (26°-29° Celcius) with the hottest months in April and early May. Surface winds in Nigeria are mainly the easterly or northeast trade winds in the dry season, and westerly in the rainy season. Bura land is no exception to this rule (Davies, 1956:18). The *harmattan*, which gives an appearance of fog and is guided by the northeast trade winds, usually appears in December and January, though it is variable. It can be thick and dusty, and may reduce visibility to about one kilometer. Thus, the climatic factor is significant, not only in relation to its effect on the character of the vegetation, but also to the dominant role it plays in determining the inhabitants' ways of life, including their patterns of economic activity.

In Bura land, the first rains are mostly experienced in March and April. The area has an average rainfall of 90 - 100 cm annually (Mshelia, 1988:10). A peak is reached at about the end of August, and the dry season begins to set in by early October.

Bura land is home to vegetation similar to that of the Northern Guinea Savannah; characterized by short grasses interspersed with stunted trees. The hills are covered with grasses; but in the frequently cultivated or permanently settled areas, useful trees have been preserved to form orchards on the hills (Udo 1970: 201). The most prominent amongst the trees are Shea butter (Bura name:*fuma; Scientific name:vitelli paradoxa), kadla - Bura name for acacia albida,* Baobab (Bura name: *kwagu; Scientific name:ndansonia digitata*), and *mbula - Bura name for tamarindus indica.* The Hawul[24] flood plains and a few streams allow for a distinctive vegetation of tall *mamzham* grass and fan palms (*mina*) to flourish. Relatively dense forests lie along some of the streams. Human activity, ranging from permanent cultivation, grazing, bush burning and exploitation of trees for fuel, has greatly altered the vegetation of the area.

The most dominant physical feature in Bura land according to Davies (1956) is the Biu Plateau. The Biu Plateau, consisting of volcanic rock, slopes off gradually and forms steep precipitous escarpments and hills. The Plateau forms fine and rugged landscapes around the Hawul River, which dissects

---

24 Hawul is the name of the major river in Bura land.

the Plateau. The Hawul is the only major river in Bura land. It flows in westward into the River Gongola and eventually into the River Benue.[25]

Spilling over the basaltic escarpment at the Plateau's edge are numerous small rivers fluctuating with the seasons and, in times of flood, producing a dazzling display of falling water at *Dzuwa* and *Tsirdludlu* Falls (Faw1973: 8).

3.3 Traditions of Origin and Migration

The available historical sources on traditions of origin and migration of the people in Bura land are based on linguistic studies and oral traditions of the Peoples. Bura land lies to the south of one of the most influential kingdoms in the history of West Africa. Originally known as Kanem,[26] the Kingdom of Borno has a long and proud history. For nearly a thousand years, Lake Chad has been the centre of the Kanuri Empire, although the seat of power moved from north to west of the Lake (Smith, 1971:156). As the Kingdom of Borno gradually moved south and west of Lake Chad, the indigenous Sau or So were dispossessed of their land, being gradually assimilated or forced to move. Adjoining the Sau were the Mbum (Usman and Alkali, 1983:221), about whom very little is known. According to one available source,

> "[t]radition holds that in the period of the first millennium A.D. all the area of the North Eastern State was peopled by these Mbum. In the period before A.D.1400 they were scattered over the area north of Benue River. But before A.D. 1200 a new people, the Jukun, numerically small but very advanced in the art of kingship migrated into the area north of Benue river, dispersed many of Mbum and left permanent mark on the remainder. Only after the decline of the Jukun power (its centre shifted south and today the Jukun live beyond Benue) did the Mbum evolve into the tribal units that today are their descendants. That is, the Mbum today formed a substratum for such tribes as the Bura, Marghi, Kilba, Higi, Gude, Fali and Bata (Faw 1973: 30)

A few recollections of Mbum connection remain today among the Bura people in places like Mbuma, Bumsa, and Buma. The Bura recall their Mbum predecessors as the Ngwi people and have traditions of pushing them southwards.

---

25   Benue is one of the two major rivers that cut across large sections of Nigeria. The other is the River Niger.

26   Kanem Bornu Empire was an empire that existed in modern Chad Republic and Nigeria from 9th century AD onward and lasted as the independent kingdom of Borno until 1900.

Another approach for determining the origin of the Bura people lies in the similarities of their language with that of Marghi, Kibaku, and Kilba. These languages are so closely related that they are often mutually intelligible. While Westerman and Bryan (1970:153) classified the languages as Chadic,[27] Greenberg (1963:46) classified them as Chad/Afro-Asiatic. Hoffmann (1963), in his study of the Bura and Marghi languages, concluded that the Bura, Marghi, Pabir, Kibaku, and Kilba share identical sound systems, morphology, syntax, and a high percentage of common vocabulary.[28]

Similarly, Meek[29] (1931) suggested that these people should all be considered as one group because they are closely related in language and custom. He further shows evidence of a wide connection between the Bura and Bantu languages of South Africa. There are striking resemblance in phonology and vocabulary with the Bantu languages. For example, literal *tl, dl, hl,* and labialised *o* and palatalised *s* are common to Bura, Zulu, and Bantu languages (Meek, 1931:137). A comparative study of thirty-one Bura root words with the Bantu group also revealed some similarities between the Bantu and Bura languages.

Meek's speculation, however, cannot be trusted. Chadic and Bantu belong to two distinct language families. Other sources, as seen earlier, suggest that the Bura seem to have originated from the extinct Mbum. But it is not possible for a group of people to come from two different areas at the same time, namely the Lake Chad area and South Africa[30]. This linguistic evidence, perhaps, indicates evidence of cultural contact between the Bura and other groups. This is surely not enough evidence to determine the origin of the people in question. If this is the case, it would not be out of place to look at the oral traditions of the Bura-speaking peoples concerning their origin.

The northern Bura-speaking peoples trace their origin to Yamta-ra-walla. According to this tradition, *mai* Idris Katargarmabe, the ruler of Borno, died in 1526, leaving the Kanuri throne vacant. Yamta, a house member of the *mai,* lost out in the succession to the throne (Cohen, 1974, 1983). Disappointed, Yamta and a few of his followers left Birnin Garzagamo, the capital of the Borno Kingdom, and came to the Bura area. On reaching Bura area, he settled at Limbur between Chikorkir and Mandiragrau. While there, some Bura for whom he became chief joined him, and he termed the new community "Pabir". Three Bura Kingdoms, namely Mandiragrau, Mirnga,

---

27 Chadic is a family of Afroasiatic tonal languages (mostly two tones) spoken in the regions west and south of Lake Chad in north central Africa.
28 All the languages mentioned are neighbouring languages.
29 A hired anthropologist by the then Nigerian colonial government to study tribes of Northern Nigeria.
30 The Bura people in this case.

and Buratai, confronted Yamta, but he fought and defeated them all. Yamta then established his kingdom.

The southern Bura speaking peoples claim origin from different places over time. For instance, the southern Bura speaking people were said to claim that they came from Asante in the west. This was based on the evidence of some copper figures found in their possession, which resemble Asante works (Temple, 1965:73). There is yet another tradition which claims origin from *rahi* (east) around the Cameroon Hills (Temple, 1965:73). According to this tradition, the southern Bura-speaking people came into their present habitat, together with the Hona and Lala groups,[31] at a time when there appeared to have been large scale migration of hill dwellers on the western slope of the Cameroon Hills long before the nineteenth century. Some southern Bura, Hona, and Lala settlements are still situated on the Hills. But the fact that some of these people lived there is not enough to suggest that they came from the Cameroon Hills. It is possible to suggest that their stay on the Hills was for defensive reasons or it could have been due to lack of available space for settlement and cultivation.

Other claims of the origin of Bura traditions point to the Lake Chad area to the north (Davies, 1956:280). What can be understood from these traditions is that they are contradictory and cannot be relied upon in determining the origin of the Bura. For example, the claim of the Asante in the west as their origin varies considerably with the claim that their origin springs from Lake Chad in the north, and also does not correspond with the claim of origin from the Cameroon Hills in the east. These divergent claims of origin from "west", "east", and "north" might perhaps need to be redefined in the context of the Bura peoples themselves. Possibly these claims may not go beyond the confines of the Lake Chad Basin or the Mandara Mountains.[32]

If it is accepted, for example, that the Lake Chad Basin area was at one time a centre of dispersal of the various peoples of Gongola - Hawul and the Upper Benue Valley, then it is possible to say with some precision that the desiccation process of the Chad Basin might have considerably helped in the north-to-south migration of peoples of the Lake (Smith, 1971:156). On the basis of this evidence, it is therefore possible to surmise that the Bura and other related groups might have been pushed southwards into their present home as a result of the desiccation of the Lake Chad Basin in the remote past.

In spite of the contradictory and conflicting nature of these traditions, they cannot be totally dismissed, for they are important pieces of evidence, perhaps, of contacts and dissection of traditions of origin.

---

31   The immediate neighbouring groups of the Bura.
32   The Mandara Mountains are a volcanic range extending about 200km along the northern part of the Cameroon-Nigeria border.

3.4 Occupation

Even though many Bura people work in both the public and private sectors of the Nigerian economy, agriculture remains the mainstay of the people to date. With high annual rainfall, low mean temperatures, thick networks of rivers and abundant fertile soil, the area remains ideal for agricultural pursuits. Popular among cultivated crops are cereals like sorghum, maize, and rice. Other crops include cotton and groundnuts, while cassava and sweet potatoes remain popular root crops cultivated in the area.

The Bura people also engage in the production of artifacts either as a specialized trade or a supplement to agriculture. Local industries like pottery, weaving, smiting, and carving are popular among the artisan population of the area. Similarly, fishing, hunting, and rearing of domestic animals supplement other trades.

3.5 Political Organization.

The northern Bura-speaking people are centralized in terms of their political organization. The Emir[33] of Biu administers the area known as an emirate. The emirate is sub-divided into districts, which are headed by a *thlerima* (district head). Each district is further divided into village units, headed by a *lawan* (village head).

In the southern Bura-speaking area, each village unit constitutes an independent political unit under the headship of the eldest established clan. The most senior of the founding clan is the *birma* (village head). The village is divided into *zara* (wards), each headed by a ward head. People of the same clan most often settle in the same area within a village unit. The most senior person of each clan is the ward head. Ward heads and the village head form a council to mediate in disputes and to discuss various village wide activities.

During the pre-colonial period, leadership was nominal and based on kinship values. Power and authority lay with the various heads of the kindred groups of clans whose functions were secular and religious. Generally, the southern Bura-speaking peoples had no tradition of loyalty or subservience to any chief of status higher than a village head. The only man with authority was the head of the family, and his authority was recognized as long as he was able to back it up by force (Davies 1956: 221). There was no overall chief of all the Bura people south of Biu. However, headmen of larger villages naturally had more prestige than those of smaller villages.

---

33 A title of high office, used particularly in a variety of places dominated by Moslems in northern Nigeria as well as in many parts of the Islamic world.

The wielding of authority as a specialized full time occupation was virtually unknown (Ajayi et. al. 1971: 72), but the eldest member of the eldest clan in the village enjoyed some degree of authority over the whole community. He was the chief of the earth cult *milim*, which sanctions communal morality and law (Davies 1956: 222).

3.6 Worldview and Religion.

Spirits[34] (*shatan*) inhabit the Bura world, and their lives are overshadowed by their fear of offending the spirits. Before the advent of Christianity, each adult possessed a personal god, the *Hyelkir*, or 'god at head' (one of the *Haptu* spirit types), usually kept in the owner's bedroom. Each compound had a household *Haptu* shrine, an important centre for worship through which protection from danger was sought. In each village, there was a *Haptu* shrine, which was publicly worshipped.

Apart from the possession of *Haptu*, there existed and to some extent still exists, the belief in an impersonal power which is possessed in a special way by certain men and animals, and at times, concentrated in objects like *mispar* (charms and amulets), *shafa* (a kind of tree), *Milim* and *Jisku* (both stone gods). They believe, too, that people and all animate beings possess *shangur*, the life principle or soul life. In many cases, the *shangur* of a wild animal is associated with a person. A person whose *shangur* is associated with a wild animal, it is said, "can have the animal still, kill or maim for him without any effort on his part. Of course, if the bush animal becomes sick or tired, he too is sick or tired and if it is killed, he likewise dies" (Bittinger 1939: 3)). This practice in particular is more common among the Kilba people living to the east of Bura land, but it is also found among the Bura people sharing borders with them.

The Bura believe that, when a person dies, he or she joins a world of ancestral spirits in which their existence is similar to life on earth, but with added wealth and joy. For a limited time after a person's death, immediate family members placate his or her ancestral spirit with sacrifices. The Bura do not, however, have a fully fledged ancestral cult—that is, one in which the ancestral spirits of both recently and long since deceased persons are routinely offered sacrifices, and in which the ancestors are perceived and

---

34 The Bura have many spirits that are known by different names, but are collectively spoken about as *shatan*. Thus, for example, the spirit connected to rivers would be referred to as *shatan kuta Hawul*, while that of hills would be referred to as *shatan Gar. Jang* is also one of the spirit types. Different characters are attributted to the spirits. Some are of good character e.g the *haptu* while some e.g. *jang* are of bad character.

treated as a major force buttressing social morality—as described in the classic accounts of Fortes (1959; 1966) and Malinowski (1954).

Above all, this belief is the belief in the supreme all-powerful deity of the Bura people, recognized under the title of *Hyel*. According to Bura folklore, *Hyel* lived near humans until their disobedience forced him to withdraw. He then became too distant to be directly influenced by human agencies, but in every act of traditional worship the name of *Hyel* is mentioned to seek help in all matters.

3.7 The Colonialization of the Bura

The contact between Europeans and the peoples of Nigeria dates back to the fifteenth century. This contact was mostly with the people who lived in some coastal areas of what is today's Southern Nigeria. It was not until the mid-nineteenth century that the British came into close contact with the peoples of the territory today referred to as Northern Nigeria. The contact between the British and the people of this region largely led their interest in developing commercial links with the Niger/Benue[35] territory, where traders from Britain had been operating for quite some time. Towards the end of the nineteenth century, a British trading concern—the National African Company—became dominant in Niger/Benue trade. The company allegedly entered into some kind of treaty with some Emirs, Chiefs and community leaders. It obtained a charter, which gave it some form of political power to administer the territories it claimed. Subsequently, the Royal Niger Company (R.N.C.), as it was known in 1899, attempted to consolidate its position through military activity in order to keep out other European rivals[36] who also had interest in the region, and to also control the numerous communities of the region. The R.N.C. charter was revoked in 1899 and the area declared a British Protectorate on January 1, 1900 (Crowder 1962: 178) with Captain (later Lord) Lugard as its High Commissioner or head of Administration.

The singular act of the 1900 proclamation was the impression it created that the British had not only taken over the administrative functions of the R. N. C., but that the people of Northern Nigeria had accepted British rule as well. This, however, was not the case because a large part of this region did not and would not accept British rule. Captain Lugard's first act in Northern Nigeria was thus tantamount to a war, which was founded on militarism. With a small army of British soldiers, supplemented by British

---

35   Niger/Benue was the name the territory around the Rivers Niger and Benue was known as during the colonial era of present Nigeria.

36   The French, Germans and Portueguse all had interest in carving out territories in different parts of Africa during the colonial era.

trained Hausa Soldiers, he attacked and subdued the emirates of Yola, Kontogora, Bida, Kano, Zaria, Sokoto, Bauchi and Katsina from 1900 to 1906.

With the conquest of these emirates, the British moved to Borno, the region where the area of study of this thesis is largely located. The occupation of Borno stemmed from the relationship between the British and the French in the Chad Basin, an area in the extreme corner of the northern part of Borno. Earlier in 1890, the two powers had reached the "say Baruwa" agreement that placed a large proportion of Borno into the British sphere of influence (Crowder 1962: 159). This agreement was later confirmed by the Anglo-French convention of 1898. However, in spite of these agreements neither the British nor French made any serious attempt to bring Borno under its effective control. The process under which Borno came under control was gradual. In 1900, the French fought Rabeh, the newly established power at Kusseri[37]. Next, the French turned to Fadel-Allah, Rabeh's son who, following the death of his father assumed leadership against the resistance to the French. The French pursued Fadel-Allah into British Borno and killed him at Gujba[38] in 1901. The British were greatly alarmed by the French pursuit of Fadel-Allah, more so when they learnt the French were collecting an indemnity of the equivalent of $80,000 from Abubakar Garbai, the legitimate Shehu of Borno, in order to restore the Elkanemi dynasty which was overthrown by Rabeh (Crowder 1962: 181). The British, fearful that most of Borno would fall into the hands of the French due to their actions, dispatched an expedition with a view to forestalling such an occurrence. The expedition, the 'Lower Borno Expedition,' consisted of 17 British officers, both political and military, 500 soldiers, 900 carriers, and 3 maxim guns (Adeleye 1971: 238), and left Ibi for Borno on the Benue River on January 23, 1902 under Colonel Morland, Commandant Northern Nigerian Regiment West Africa Frontier Force. Morland's main task was to investigate the killing of Fadel-Allah by the French troops at Gujba. It was later found to be true. As a result, he stationed a company of troops at Gujba and proceeded to Maiduguri where Captain Cochrane was left with some troops to safeguard British interests, pending the establishment of a British administration in the area. The British did not have to fight in Borno since they promised Shehu Garbai the throne if he would cease paying the indemnity demanded by the French and submit to British rule, a proposal he gladly accepted. He was eventually established as the Shehu[39] of Borno.

British contact with the Bura people was first recorded in 1904. In that year, a military officer, Mr. Lawrence, came to Biu with troops from Gujba (Biu Dist. 417: 5-6, N.N.A.K.). He visited the Pabir chief, Garga Kwamting,

---

37 Kusseri is located near Lake Chad in Cameroon.
38 Gujba is in present Yobe State of Nigeria.
39 The traditional title of the ruler of the Elkanemi dynasty.

at his residence at Pelaminta. Although the purpose of his visit was not known, it became apparent from his actions that the British were prepared to take the Bura country by force of arms if necessary. To make his intentions clear, Mr. Lawrence demonstrated the power of the gun against a tree (Davies 1956: 43). His action was a clear sign that the British were prepared to forcefully impose their rule in Bura land. However, the people were not prepared to willingly accept British rule. This led to the dispatching of a number of patrol troops in the area. From 1907 to 1918, no less than ten military patrols were undertaken by the British to bring the area under their effective control.

In 1907, with the approval of the Borno resident, Mr. Hewby, the first British patrol into Bura land was undertaken. The patrol was designed to bring the Pabir, Bura and Tera areas under the effective control of the Pabir chief Garga Kwamting, who was earlier (1904) singled out and installed by the British as a third class 'Chief of Pabirs' at Magumeri, near Maiduguri (Davies 1956: 48). The British hoped to secure control of Bura country with this patrol by increasing the power and influence of Garga Kwamting. At the end of the 1907 patrol, the villages of Debarfu and Paratatabu were attacked and burnt, respectively.

In 1908, another punitive patrol was dispatched to the hilly Bura areas south of Biu. Due to the topography of this part of the country, patrolling was not possible. The people of the area fiercely resisted the subjugation of their territory under the Pabir chief. The administrative records of 1909 put it thus:

"The true Bura were not subdued by the Pabir and have led a largely independent existence upon their hills until now, but it is proposed to slowly group the whole district under Mai/Chief at Biu where it is hoped there will be less necessity for military patrol paying visit there every year as it occurs now (cited in Davies 1956: 57).

In spite of the difficulties encountered by the British on Bura land, Garga Kwamting was eventually installed as chief over both the 'Buras and Pabirs' in 1908. For the next eleven years, the Bura villages south of Biu pitted their strength against the British. They presented a great deal of resistance to the Pabir chief who had been imposed upon them and who was supposed to be in charge of them. They did not took orders from him or anyone else, including the British. As a result of the stiff resistance put up by the Bura, Davies (1956) concluded that the Bura people did not wish for British administration in their area because it interfered with their independence and tribal 'orgies'.

Despite the resistance by the Bura, the British nonetheless dispatched another patrol to Bura land in 1909. This patrol was the largest ever recorded in the history of Bura people. It consisted of 190 men and 6 European officers, and Biu was made their base. The patrol made a circular tour of

Bura land and about 240 villages were visited. The British were said to have lost 15 men, killed 10 and captured 20 (Davies 1956: 60).

A year after this patrol, the British reached Garkida in 1910, the largest Bura village in the extreme south of Bura territory from Biu. That year, there was a great deal of hostility expressed against a British officer sent to the village. A group of soldiers were sent to Garkida to suppress the uprising. The whole village was burnt and several people were captured and put on trail. At the end, only two men of the village's ruling family[40] were convicted and taken to Lokoja as prisoners (Yola, Prof. G2. R, N.N.A.K.). Each served a jail term of no less than 10 years (Bettinger 1938: 85). Even then it could not be said that the British had subdued the whole Bura area. It was not until 1918 that the entire Bura land had been finally subdued. From 1918 to 1933, British administration in the area was not easy to implement; thereby leading to the area being designated as an "unsettled area" (Biu Dist. 259, N.N.A.K.), meaning that it was unsafe for the British and other European nationals to traverse. However, this does not mean that the area was peopled by an "uncontrollable" group, but simply that the Bura had a strong pride in their independence which made them reluctant to submit to any foreign control either from within or outside their own system. The British failed to realize this fact, thus making it difficult for the establishment of its colonial rule in the area.

However, in trying to establish some form of administration among the southern Bura speaking peoples, the British, in accordance with their policy of 'indirect rule', naturally looked for a powerful chief through whom they could administer the area. Since the Bura people do not have a centralized form of political organization—meaning they had no overall chief—the British arbitrarily singled out the Pabir chief, Garga Kwamting, in 1904 as the most viable instrument of indirect rule among the Bura. The British evolved a policy of extending his authority and power until he was in charge of the Bura, Pabir, and Tera areas in what is now the Biu Emirate (Mshelia 1983: 18). From 1908 to 1918, these people were progressively placed under the rule of the emerging emirate at Biu. The result of this forceful incorporation as noted above, was a series of armed confrontations and village burnings in which the Bura were unwillingly made to accept Pabir, and above all, British rule. In several cases, Bura village headmen were arrested and brought to trail in Biu where they were given jail sentences (Biu Dist. H.9 N.N.A.K.). For the Pabir, this period represented the utilization of British power to expand their control over all Bura speaking areas. For the Bura, it represented a war of resistance against colonialism and the unwanted rule of Biu over a previously independent people with a completely different form of political organization. Some acceded to this rule, while others migrated

---

40 The Tarfa clan.

across the Hawul River into the Garkida area in order to avoid the Pabir and British rule. The majority of the Buras that fled to Garkida were subsequently placed under the Fulani emir of Adamawa.[41] Since then, the Bura people have remained divided among the neighbouring emirates of Biu and Yola. From 1910 to 1924, several attempts were made by the British to integrate the Bura of Garkida with the Bura in Biu, the neighbouring Western Marghi, Ga'anda and the Whona people for administrative purposes.

In 1914, S.H.P. Vereker suggested in his assessment report the amalgamation of the Bura and the Whona people into one sub-district – "The Whona-Bura Sub-district" (Yola Prof. G.2. U, N.N.A.K). According to this arrangement the sub-district head appointed was Giyaye, a Whona chief who was requested by the Bura of the Sub-district. The Bura realized that their unit in Adamawa was too small to form a convenient administration. Besides, the Whona had given them shelter in their flight from Biu. They preferred to remain with the Whona than to be re-amalgamated with division of the Pabir in Biu.

Under the new administrative re-organization, Garkida was placed under the district of Giola (Yola Prof. G.2.S. N.N.A.K.) that was ruled by a Fulani chief who had the hereditary right of appointing chiefs in the district. In 1917, the resident colonial officer in charge of Ga'anda District II K. V. Elphistone approved Jauro Goila's appointment of Yerima Dzankar as the headman of Garkida (Yola Prof. G.2.S. N.N.A.K.). Yerima Dzankar was perhaps the most influential of all the chiefs of the trans-Hawul Buras, but several of the people within the region questioned his right to leadership of the region. However, with his appointment as the village head of Garkida, indirect rule could thus be said to have been established in the area. Yet, by placing the Garkida unit under the Fulani District head of Goila, the British did not only undermine the Bura system of political organization, but had also contradicted the 'minimal interference' and 'use of the existing institution' as enshrined within the Indirect Rule System (Cameron 1934: 2-3).

Lugard took a firm stand in regards to the 'non-Moslem government'. He maintained that it was not part of colonial government policy to force independent "pagans" under Fulani rule, no matter how efficient that rule might be. The British aim, according to him, was to develop the institutions of "pagan" tribes however rudimentary they might be, until they became self-governing communities in the same way as the Moslem state (Perham 1937:134). Lugard's political staff did not strictly adhere to his administrative policies. H. R. Palmer, for instance, confessed that Lugard's political memoranda were neither laws nor conscious policy (Haussler 1968: 60) and were soon out of date. Perham, however, argued that the defiance on the part of the political staff was as a result of their success in developing a special

---

41   An emirate in present Adamawa State of Nigeria with headquarters in Yola town.

type of administration in the large emirates, a system which they were determined to extend wholesale over to non-Moslem areas where it had no foundations (Perham 1937: 142). It was doubly alien to the non-Moslem, especially the southern Bura speaking peoples, not only in that it was Islamic, but also in that the institution of district head and even village head often bore little relation to their clan organization in which emphasis was based upon conciliatory rather than autocratic authority.

The year 1921 was also significant for administrative re-organization between Biu and Adamawa emirates. The trans-Hawul Buras who had been under Yola Province were transferred back to the Biu division in the month of October, partly because they were of the same tribe with Biu Buras, but mainly because their area was not yet under effective administrative control and had become a sanctuary for "Bura criminals" from Biu (Davies 1956: 78). The Biu divisional administration had been complaining about the Buras crossing into Yola Province after they had committed criminal acts. The territory, which was transferred to Biu, consisted of a strip of country running along the south bank of the River Hawul from Lokoja to Garkida, about 4.8 kilometers. These areas were organized into three villages, Garkida, Gobla, and Lokoja, under the name 'South Bura District', with headquarters at Pelaciroma, near Garkida. Lawan Betara Pela, a Pabir, was appointed as the district head (Davies 1956: 78, Biu Dist. 417, N.N.A.K.). This organization did not last long and in April 1923, the 'South Bura District' was re-organized into the 'East Bura District' with its headquarters at Kwajaffa. In 1924, Garkida and Gobla units were transferred back to Adamawa Province. This was largely due to the commencement of missionary work by missionaries from the Church of the Brethren in America in Garkida[42] (cf. Chapter 7).

3.8   The Bura as Subject of Anthropological and Linguistic Research

With the exception of some works by colonial administrators and missionaries, hardly any ethnographic work exists about the Bura. To the best of my knowledge, the studies that do exist appeared only after the colonialization and missionization of the area. The studies bear the clear characteristics of first descriptions, presenting surveys of language, political structure and economy of Bura land (Temple 1919 [2nd edition 1965]; Meek 1931; Helser 1926, 1934; Bittinger 1921, 1939; Davies 1956; Kulp 1968; Baldwin 1973; Thomasson 1973). However, in the 1970s, scholarly works that go beyond

---

42   Missionary work commenced at Garkida in 1923.

descriptions of the political system of the southern Bura speaking peoples emerged. Cohen (1974, 1977, 1983,1988) wrote extensively on the Pabir and Bura political systems, the former having a centralized system and the later described as acephalous/stateless. His focus, though, was more on the Bura being devoid of any central form of government. Interestingly, having come into contact with western education early, Bura scholars themselves have published little ethnographic research on the Bura.

The Bura language, in contrast, became important as a subject of study by linguists through the activities of a mission station in Garkida, which has published school materials in the vernacular. Bura Primers were developed and published soon after the commencement of Christian missionary activities in the area for the purpose of teaching western education. Also, the New Testament of the Bible, a Hymnal book, and several other Christian texts were translated into the Bura language for the purpose of evangelizing the area. Apart from the Primers and the translated materials, many linguists (Hoffmann 1955, Blench 1999, 2009, Maddieson 1983, Muazu 2010, Hartmann 2007, 2012,) have published on various aspects of Bura language.

3.9 Conclusion

This chapter has attempted to present a wider context for the Bura. It gives the environmental and historical context of Bura land and its people. The issues discussed in the chapter are factors that contributed to shaping a Bura worldview and how the encounter with colonialists set into motion changes; particularly in the way in which society was organized. Some of the changes that occurred in combination with other factors have had a significant impact on some indigenous practices of the people as will be discussed in the case of the *tsinza* tradition in subsequent chapters of this thesis.

4   The Bura *Tsinza* Xylophone

4.1   Introduction

Xylophones are found throughout Africa, Central and South America, Southeast Asia (mainland and insular), the Marquesas Island in Polynesia and Melanesia. In Europe, xylophones are used in the traditional music of Austria, the Czech Republic, Hungary and more. Hornbostel and Sachs (1933) classified the xylophone as an idiophone and divided it into two major types: those with bedded keys and those with suspended keys. However, with the advancement of ethnomusicological research over the last few decades, scholars have developed several local systems of classifying musical instruments that are based on different principles than those of the western system that was established by E. M. Hornbostel and Curt Sachs. Maxwell (1999) argues that Hornbostel and Sachs' system of classifying musical instruments, first by the principal resonating material and then by the type of materials and action used to set the sound in motion, does not cover all types of xylophone found in West Africa. This is, according to her, because the gourds are not the primary resonating material even though they are an essential part of the sound aesthetics of West African xylophones. Rather, as she puts it, "in most local classification systems, the number of keys, pitch areas (that is pitches that cluster around distinct registers such as bass or soprano), and the performance context and function are essential criteria for categorizing xylophone types" in West Africa (Maxwell 1999: 64).

Xylophones exist in different shapes and forms. Materials such as wood, bamboo, logs or tubes may be used to construct it. All it requires to construct a xylophone are a material for the base, such as wood, and the 'keys', which are supported at two nodes of vibration, which also must be tuned. Resonators for the instrument also come in different forms. It may be a pit or a trough, a gourd, a clay pot or cow horn. In some cases, individual resonators are attached to each key. Individual keys may be fixed temporarily or permanently to a support or they may be loose. The keys may rest on a pit or trough suspended between supports, on straw bundles, or banana stems; or they may rest on the legs or thighs of a player. A thick roll of grass, rubber or plastic knobs, or a strip of cloth may be used as an insulator to allow free vibration of the keys. Based on the above explanations, this chapter focuses on the Bura *tsinza* xylophone. The chapter starts with a review of some of the works of the scholars who have studied the instrument in Africa. Attention is paid to situating the *tsinza* in the context of other African xylophones with a similar order of keys, and distinguishing what makes it unique compared to the ones found in the continent, and particularly in the northeast region of Nigeria.

4.2 The Tsinza in the Context of Other African Xylophones

The xylophone is a wide spread instrument found in many countries in Africa. It exists in a variety of forms and is played in many different ways. It also serves different musical functions in the areas in Africa where it is found.

To the best of my knowledge, there are not many recent studies on the xylophone in Africa. However, available literature – many of which relates more to Anglophone Africa[43] - (Yoo Jin Bae 2001; Heather A. Maxwell 1999; Olga Boone 1936; P. R. Kirby 1953; A. M. Jones 1959; Gerhard Kubik 1960, 1964, 1969, 1985; Klaus P. Wachsmann 1971; L. Anderson 1967; J. H. Kwabena Nketia 1974) seems to be more concerned with details such as tuning and distribution of the instrument. Little or no attention at all is paid to the social context of the instrument in most of the available literature. Many of the studies likewise focus on the xylophones found in Southern, East, and Central Africa rather than those in West Africa.

Some of the scholars cited earlier have plotted the distribution of the xylophone on a maps of Africa, according to the different types of construction. However, a closer look at such maps provided in their works does not feature the Bura xylophone type. It also does not fit into any of the types of the xylophones described in their studies of the instrument in Africa.

Bae (2001) examines the distribution, construction, tuning, and performance of the African log xylophone. The log xylophone is one of the subcategories of xylophones in Africa. It is unique because it is mainly identified by the lack of a resonator attachment. Wooden slabs rest on pieces of wood, bundles of grass, or banana stems which commonly serve as the support frames. He observed in his work that due to the unusual distribution of the xylophone in the African continent, some scholars tend to suggest Asian origins for the African xylophone. The Ugandan *amadinda* xylophone is presented as the representative log xylophone in his study. However, like many of the early scholars who worked on xylophones in Africa before him, attention was only paid to tuning, construction, and playing technique.

Maxwell (1999) focuses on the use of the xylophone among the Mande and Voltaic peoples who live in the savannah regions of West Africa. She discusses the history, distribution, terminology, and tunings of the xylophone. Her primary focus, though, is how individuals interact with the instrument. For her, learning about xylophone music culture provides a window into the diverse complexity of West African societies and worldviews. She not only drew on the personal narratives of musicians to discuss tuning,

---

43   This includes five countries in West Africa: The Gambia, Sierra Leone, Liberia, Ghana and Nigeria, as well as a part of Cameroon.

classification, and performance aesthetics, but also uses their voice to explain how the instrument "speaks" with the human and spiritual world at performance events. Similar to Maxwell's study, this thesis will look heavily into understanding the tsinza in its traditional context. Her work will serve as one of the principal references, particularly when trying to understand how the Bura instrument "speaks" with the ancestral and human world.[44]

Boone (1936) studies xylophones in the Belgian Congo (now the Democratic Republic of Congo). She distinguishes two types of xylophone: those with free keys and those with permanently fixed keys. She further subdivided the ones with permanently fixed keys into those with and without resonators. Her interest clearly lay with the ways in which keys and resonators were attached or mounted, tuning patterns, terminologies, and distribution of xylophone types in her area of study and in other areas of Africa.

Kirby (1953) studied the musical instruments of South Africa with the aim of offering specific and detailed information on the subject. One of the instruments he studied is the resonated xylophone, which he describes as the most elaborate musical instrument found in South Africa. According to him, the xylophone is commonly called the *marimba*. Two varieties are known, one belonging to the Venda and the other among the Tshopi. Both varieties are known by the same name *mbila,* and are constructed on the same principles. Kirby attempts to trace the origins of the *mbila* and describes in detail its construction and tuning. He also describes how both groups play the instrument.

Jones (1959) explores the evidence for cultural influence with regard to the xylophone in Africa stemming from Indonesia. He built his arguments around samples of evidence on equidistance tuning, geographical distribution, similarities in construction, and cultural practices. He compared certain aspects of the xylophone, such as (1) seven-note equal temperament appearing at the same pitch in Cambodia, Java, East Africa, West Africa and the Congo; (2) five-note equal temperament in Java, the Congo, West Africa, Uganda; and (3) singing in parallel thirds in the Gulf of Guinea, the Congo Basin, on the east coast opposite Madagascar, in Madagascar, Sumatra, the Philippines and Tonga. Even though his study favours Asian origin for the African xylophone, he did not provide enough evidence to prove his claims.

Kubik (1960, 1964, 1969, and 1985) examines the music of the southern kingdoms of Uganda. The xylophone was the key instrument of his studies of the music of these kingdoms. He was an apprentice to one of the Kabaka's court musicians and learned to play the *amadinda* and *akadinda* xylophones of Buganda first hand in order to have a better understanding

---

44   The Bura believe that the living "speak" with the *mambula* soul of a deceased member of their society through the *tsinza.*

of the structure of the music. In his studies, he concerned himself primarily with information concerning the types of Ganda xylophone, their compass and tuning, tone systems, techniques of performance, melodies used, and the matter of rhythm and its build-up in a full performance. It is clear from all the studies he undertook on the xylophone that his interest was placed more on technical issues than on the social context of the instrument amongst the groups he studied.

Wachsman (1971) examined musical instruments in the Kiganda tradition and their place in the East African scene. Prominent among the instruments he discusses are the different types of xylophone found among the Kiganda. These are the twelve-key xylophone, *entaala* or *amadinda* and the large xylophone, the *akadinda*. He briefly attempted a description of some of the customs associated with the *entaala*. However, his description focuses more so on the distribution of the different types of the instrument and its current form at the time of his study. He explained that it was beyond the scope of his paper to describe in detail the customs associated particularly with the lager xylophones, *akadinda*. Nevertheless, his observation on a possible change in the dance style to the music of the instrument is of interest to this thesis, even though the focus is not on dance. He clearly describes a case of change and continuity, a theme which is especially important in the case of the *tsinza*. He wrote:

"The movements, executed in a counter clockwise circle, were gentle and shuffling, with slow and apparently relaxed muscular action, utterly different from the attack and tempo of the manner that prevails today..." As for the modern style, it demands, "tossing the head, jerking the neck, making the chest dance, dancing as if walking slowly, and looking back as if in fright" (Wachsman 1971: 111).

Anderson (1967) describes the various types of xylophones she encountered during her stay in Uganda for three years and reassesses their distribution across East Africa. She observes, "musical instruments often have specific roles in African societies, intimately bound up with the lives and traditions of its people" (Anderson 1967: 46). Her assertion holds true for the tsinza. Despite this statement, Anderson's study gives little attention to the socio-cultural context of the people whom she studied. Her interest was clearly on the varieties of structural form found in the xylophone type used across East Africa and of the different methods used for playing the instrument. By contrast, this thesis takes Anderson's statement to heart and focuses on the role the instrument plays in the lives of the Bura people, as well as the changes it has undergone as a result of the changing social situations.

The *gyil*, a type of xylophone, is an instrument that is greatly revered by the Lobi/Dagara people of Ghana, and is perhaps the most studied in

West Africa (Strumpf 1970, 1976; Aning 1989; Bragner 1993; Mensah 1967a, 1967b, 1993; Saighoe 1984; Vercelli 2006; Wiggins and Joseph 1992). Xylophones related to the *gyil* and played by groups considered to be the cousins of the Lobi/Dagara, the Sissala and Birifor, have also been studied (Seavoy 1982; Godsey 1980; 1984). The *gyil* is used primarily to announce death in the communities. It is a fourteen-key instrument usually played in pairs. It is made of hard wood called *liga* suspended over a wooden frame, below which hang calabash gourds that serve as the resonators. Small holes in the gourds are covered by Spider web silk to produce a buzzing sound. For the fastenings, antelope sinew and leather are used. The instrument is played with rubber-headed wooden mallets.

There are different types of *gyil*, depending on the social context in which the music is played. Some *gyils* are made for playing at funerals; others are for initiation rituals, and others for secular purposes. Though different in terms of construction compared to the *tsinza*, the *gyil* is an important instrument that is also used in funerals by the Lobi/Dagara. The various studies by different scholars are therefore of considerable importance to this thesis. Many of the studies not only considered the construction and tuning of the *gyil*, but also the variety of social contexts within which it is used.

Nketia (1974) describes three types of xylophones found among African societies:

"First, graded series of wooden slabs or keys mounted over a resonance chamber such as a pit, a box or trough or a clay pot. Pit xylophones are found in in few places in West Africa (Guinea, Nigeria and Chad), in the Central African Republic (among the Azande and Kala), and in Kenya (among the Kusu). Box xylophones are played by the Zaramo of Tanzania, while xylophone keys tied over pots are found in Ibo land in Nigeria. In the second type of xylophones, the keys are laid over two pieces of banana stems and are kept in position by sticks affixed to the stem between the keys – common in W. Africa (for example in Kissi country in Guinea and in the Ivory Coast), as well as in Central and Eastern Africa (e.g. Democratic Republic of Congo, Uganda, Tanzania and Mozambique. The third type has keys mounted over a wooden frame below which a number of gourd resonance are suspended, graded in size relation to the pitches of the wooden slabs. It has a wide distribution in W. Africa, as well as in central and eastern Africa – Democratic Republic of Congo to Mozambique and further south to Vendaland" (Nketia 1974: 81).

The Bura xylophone *tsinza* and indeed those of its closest neighbours, the Ga'anda and Tera, do not fit into any of the descriptions given by Nketia. Compared with other xylophones found in Africa and particularly in the region, the *tsinza* is unique. Two specific qualities mark it as unique in the African context, especially in regards to the particular technique of playing this instrument: the Y-shaped, forked stick and the order of the keys. The shape of the sticks enables the player to beat either one or two keys simultaneously. But the player would only play certain plates together which, in turn, determines the uniqueness of their arrangement.

Both the Tera and Ga'anda people live within the same neighbourhood as the Bura. Today, the Ga'anda xylophone (*kilaya*) has seven keys made of wood, and under each key is a cattle horn of a particular length that serves as a resonating chamber. The *kilaya* originally had gourds as resonators, but they were substituted with cattle horns at some point (Berns 1985: 43). The *kilaya* was originally a five to seven fixed-key xylophone with gourd resonators played together at funeral ceremonies in the presence of the corpse laid out on a wooden bier. Even though the *kilaya* nowadays seem to be similar to the *tsinza*, there are some differences. Unlike the *tsinza*, it is played on the ground and never suspended from the musician's shoulders during dance occasions. The *kilaya* also has a very different tone from that of the *tsinza*. It does not make the buzzing sound that the *tsinza* makes when it is played. This may in part be due to the fact that the Ga'anda do not cut the tips of the resonating horns under the xylophone keys and attach spider web as the Bura do. The spider web gives the *tsinza* its buzzing effect (see 4.4 below on construction of the instrument).

The main instrument of Tera dance bands is the xylophone, which they call *shinji*. The *shinji* is played a bit differently from the *tsinza*, but the distinctions are not nearly as clear as those between the Bura and Ga'anda xylophones. Boja (personal communication, 2003) insists that the Tera people do not make their own *shinji*. Rather, they buy it from the Bura. Perhaps this could be one of the reasons that the distinction between the Bura *tsinza* and the Tera *shinji* is so miniscule.

Further away from the Bura, Tera and Ga'anda regions, xylophones are also found amongst the Jukun of Taraba State and the Birom people of Plateau State, both in Nigeria.[45] The Jukun xylophone is similar to that of the Bura. Indeed, in one of the several versions of the Bura Nganjiwa clan (clan associated more with the *tsinza*) tradition of origin, they partly claim their origin in the Jukun. While narrating the version of the tradition that claims origin from the Jukun, Boja states:

"The origin of the Nganjiwa people is Wukari. We are Jukun people from Wukari. Our forefather came from that place and settled at Yabal... Our forefather came with his traditional rites from Wukari, from the Jukun people. He came with it right to this village and practiced it here." (Boja, personal communication, 2003)

---

45   Taraba is in the Northeast while Plateau is in the middle belt of Nigeria.

Furthermore, Boja claimed that there is no difference between the Bura and Jukun xylophone both in terms of its construction and the tunes played. He narrated a story of how he met a Jukun man in Ibadan (Southern Nigeria) to show that the Jukun and Bura xylophones are the same:

> "I knew this when I went to Ibadan. It was in 1971. It was when Yakubu Gowon was the Head of State. There was a Jukun man. He came from Wukari. He was a DPO (Divisional Police Officer). While I was playing the *tsinza*, he came and collected the beaters from me. He then asked, "Where are you from?" I said, "I am from Biu." "You are from Biu?" I said yes. "What is your clan name?" I said, "I am Nganjiwa" "If you are Nganjiwa, where is your origin?" I said, "I am from Jukun land." He said, "We are the Jukuns." He just started playing the *tsinza* exactly the way I played it... Yes... even the traditional tunes that used to be played in the past. He started talking to me about it. We became friends because of this. We met again at a festival in Lagos. Our friendship continued. Again we met in Kaduna. Here too, we continued to be friendly. But he is a Jukun man. He came from Wukari. But now we have not seen each other for more than ten years. Whether he is still alive, only God knows. Yes, in our own case the playing of music started with our great – grandfathers then it spread to us." (Boja, personal communication, 2003)

The Bura and Jukun xylophones, however, are not exactly the same as claimed by Boja. The Jukun xylophone also has seven keys, but the organological structure[46] is different. Furthermore, it is played in a different manner compared to that of the Bura t*sinza*.

Xylophones are also found among the Birom people of Plateau State of Nigeria. The Birom *Kudung* xylophone is completely different from the Bura *tsinza* in terms of size and construction, though the materials used are similar. However, the *Kudung* has fourteen keys and it is not played with Y-shaped beaters, as is in the case of the Bura.

Among the Igbo of Southeast Nigeria, there are two general groups of xylophones. The first group consists of small instruments with a limited number of keys, often two. The keys are attached to the top of an open clay pot. The attachment is done by means of a peg at each end, but at the same time separated from the pot by a woven grass collar. The second group consist of those that have resonators, which are either a gourd or a box. The Igbo xylophones are completely different from the Bura *tsinza*.

The differences identified between the *tsinza* and those of its neighbours, and indeed those of other groups in Nigeria, make the Bura instrument

---

46 The order of the keys is not the same as that of the Bura *tsinza,* which has ist lowest key right in the middle. The Jukun xylophone does not have its lowest key in the middle, but more to the right in the arrangement of the keys.

quite unique not only in the region but also in the African context. Of all the studies carried out on the xylophone in Africa, none has identified xylophones with a similar order of keys. In the sections that follow, the Bura *tsinza* will be discussed in detail vis-à-vis its oral history, construction, construction and its language, decoration and its meaning, organological description, and regional differences in construction and decoration

4.3 Tsinza – Oral History

With the exceptions of a few writings[47] by colonial officers (Davies 1956, Meek 1931), no literature exists on Bura music. One of the instruments mentioned in these accounts is the *tsinza*. The little that had been written on the *tsinza* does not mention anything about its history; however, what do exist are oral histories.

The following oratures on the history of the *tsinza* are quoted from interviews with Musa Kanjalma, Hamza Nganjiwa and Audu Bata, all famous *tsinza* players.[48] From their narration it appears that there are many legends about the origin of the Bura Xylophone *tsinza*. The first legend links the origin of the *tsinza* with the transitional period of the development from a hunter-gatherer society to an agricultural society. Kanjalma, a renowned *tsinza* player recounts:

"Once upon a time, there were two brothers living in the same place. They gathered their foodstuff in the forest and ate everything raw. One night one of them had a dream. The following morning he told his brother that in his dream he had learnt how to light fire; and he took a piece of wood and a stem of guinea-corn plant and demonstrated what he had done in his dream. Suddenly flames leapt up. His brother bought the fire from him. With the help of the fire, he succeeded in producing a metal hoe, which he used to clear the bush for his guinea-corn farm. So, this very year he brought home an extremely good harvest. He and his children were very happy. In the evening they were sitting and laughing together but did not know what to play to express their happiness.

Then their father went back into the forest and cut some dry wood. One piece slipped from his hand, fell down and struck a most beautiful sound. The father paused! He picked up the piece, cut it a bit and dropped it again. Now the sound was even better. He shortened the wood and gathered another six pieces, which he treated in the same way. In the evening after dinner, they

---

47 Mostly colonial reports and notes on the cultures of ethnic groups in territories under administrators appointed by the colonial government.
48 Widely known in Bura land because of their skills in playing the *tsinza*.

were sitting together again. The father took out the seven pieces of wood, tied them together, rested them between his knees and played for his children to dance. He made one for his brother as well who took it home to also play for his children.

When the children grew up, they decided to improve the instrument of their fathers. However, their knowledge about the construction of a xylophone grew slowly. One of the boys held a wooden key in front of the mouth of a clay pot; but he realized the sound did not improve. Then he took a calabash; that sounded nice, but unfortunately the calabash broke later. That is how the tsinza became what we are playing today." (Kanjalma, personal communication, 1989)

Apart from linking this legend of the origin of the *tsinza* with the transitional period of the development from hunter-gatherer society to a cultivating one, 'non-natural' characters[49] are seen at play here as well. First, a dream led to the creation of fire that in turn led to the production of the hoe – an important implement for the largely agrarian Bura society – and subsequently cultivation of crops resulting in a bumper harvest. Second, a bumper harvest led to the search and 'accidental' discovery of a musical instrument, which a family, that did not know what to 'play' to celebrate its success, used to entertain itself.

In the dream, the man saw himself make a fire. For the Bura this is not natural. Though the Bura do not have a fully fledged ancestral cult—one in which the ancestral spirits of both recently and long ago deceased persons are routinely offered sacrifices, and in which the ancestors are perceived and treated as a major force buttressing social morality—as described in the classic accounts of Fortes (1959; 1966) and Malinowski (1954), many things considered 'unnatural' are associated with the ancestors. The idea of the fire in the dream in a Bura worldview would be considered as having been given by the ancestors. As is the thought of going into the forest and cutting a piece of wood, which accidentally slipped from the hand, fell down and struck the ground, creating a most beautiful sound.

From this legend, it could be seen as an attempt to portray the *tsinza* as a musical instrument that was created by the spiritual world and given to the people. In the interview with Boja cited earlier, he emphasized that the *tsinza* was passed down to the people from their great-grandfathers, whom he linked with the Jukuns, an ethnic group that has a similar xylophone. The legend also talks about how the children improved upon it, an indication of the process of how the instrument came to be what it is today.

Another legend links the origin of the *tsinza* to a *Cicu*.[50] According to this legend, as narrated by Hamza Nganjiwa:

---

49   Characters existing outside of or not in accordance with nature.
50   One of the Bura spirit types.

"One day *Cicu* was playing the *tsinza* while seated alone inside a certain river. He was sitting on the riverbed. A certain man of the Nganjiwa clan who was on his way to the river to have a bath heard the music of the *tsinza* and wondered what sort of instrument sounded that nice. He became curious and decided to have a look at who was playing the instrument. From the banks of the river he saw the *Cicu* playing the instrument. He hid himself and observed what he was doing. After playing for a while the *Cicu* stopped playing and kept the *tsinza* aside. He went into the water of the river to have a bath. As he was bathing, the Nganjiwa man came out from his hiding to have his bath too. He hurriedly finished his bath and when he noticed that the *Cicu* did not notice his presence, he picked the *tsinza* together with the beaters and run away with it. This was how the *tsinza* became the instrument of the people of Nganjiwa clan." (Nganjiwa, personal communication, 2003).

Spirits, as earlier mentioned, inhabits the Bura world and their lives are overshadowed by their fear of offending the spirits. However, spirits are categorized into two: good and bad spirits. It is interesting to note that the word *Cicu* in the Bura language connotes 'madness' as well, since *Cicu* specifically refers to a person who has a psychiatric problem in modern medicine. Such a person is considered as being possessed by bad spirits, spirits that guide him or her to be violent and destructive. Similarly, a person who is knowledgeable[51] and does something that is considered to be 'unnatural' is also referred to as *Cicu*. Such a person is seen as being possessed and guided by good spirits. Therefore, all happenings that are considered to be super-natural in all aspects of Bura life (e.g. traditional medicine for the curing of diseases, discovery of new farm implements, etc.) are considered to be guided by the good spirits. Some of the "super-natural" happenings might be carried out directly by a *Cicu* or it could be done through a person it chooses to possess in order to carry out a task.

The *Cicu* encountered by the Nganjiwa man in the second legend is thought to be a good one. It is thought to be a good one because it brought the *tsinza* for the people. Owing to the fear the Bura have of spirits, the Nganjiwa man had to 'steal' the *tsinza* while *Cicu* was still in the river bathing. The narrator of this legend explained to me that it is not as if *Cicu* did not realize what was happening (i.e. the *tsinza* being stolen). But because the instrument was meant for the people, *Cicu* allowed the man to take it. However, because of the fear some of the Bura still have for *Cicu* today, whenever the *tsinza* is carried across a stream or a river,[52] a note must be

---

51 Particularly having skills that comes from experience and is creative.
52 There are many streams and rivers intersecting many parts of Bura land; where transportation between villages is mainly on foot crossing one or more may be required.

struck at intervals on the instrument for the duration of the crossing. This is done to appease *Cicu*. The Bura still fear that the Cicu must have been offended by the manner in which the instrument was "stolen."

Again, like in the first one, this legend tries to portray the *tsinza* as coming from a non-natural source. *Cicu*, being the spirit, created the instrument and its music, and gave it to the Bura people.

Another legend traced the origin of the *tsinza* to an earlier type made out of sorghum (guinea-corn) stalks.[53] This is the legend as narrated by Audu Bata, another renowned *tsinza* player:

"The *tsinza* as we know it today was developed from an earlier type made out of guinea cornstalks. Our great grandfather, the man that founded our clan, was a man of many talents. He gathered some pieces of the corn stalks, broken from its joints. He stroked each one to determine the sound they produced and selected seven pieces that have different sounds. He then tied them together putting a big one next to a smaller one. He memorized the sound of each and where he placed them. He collected two other pieces of cornstalks, which he used as beaters for playing the instrument. He taught his children how to play the instrument. This very first instrument served as their instrument for a period of time. It became apparent that the *tsinza* made of cornstalk was not strong and cannot last long enough. An idea came to him to instead use wood to make the instrument to replace the one earlier made. He went into the forest and cut some pieces of *Angilma* (African Ebony) tree. He cut several pieces from the wood. It was, however, difficult for him to determine the sounds of the seven pieces of wood he needed. He then peeled off the bark of the wood. He dug a hole in which he poured in some sand. He arranged the pieces of wood on the sand inside the hole and covered them with another layer of sand. He gathered from his farm *congcong* (guinea-corn chaff) and dried wood and piled it on top of the buried wood and set fire to it. The fire was left to burn for some time so that the sap of the wood would be dried out. He dug out the pieces of wood when after the fire had been put out and the whole thing left to cool down for some days. He stroked each of the woods after bringing it out of the hole and selected the seven pieces he need for the *tsinza*. This was how the *tsinza* came into being." (Bata, personal communication, 2003).

This legend appears to be different from the earlier ones. From the surface, it doesn't seem to directly attribute the origin of the *tsinza* to some non-natural forces. Instead, nature seems to be seen at work here. However, the mere fact that the idea came from the narrator's "great-grandparents" may mean that the ancestors provided it. So, the Bura would still see it

---

53 Sorghum (guinea-corn) is the staple food of the Bura people. It is cultivated by every farmer and there is an aboundance of the stalks everywhere.

as something coming from the ancestral land, therefore, linking it with a non-natural character.

Like the first legend though, it appears to link the origin of the instrument to the transformation from hunter-gatherer society to a cultivation society as well. The materials used came directly from cultivated sorghum by the ancestors of the narrator of the legend. This legend also portrays the instrument as something created out of nature and given to the people for their use by a non-natural character—their ancestors.

All the above legends about the origin of the *tsinza* seem to be very popular amongst the *tsinza* players in the various Bura communities. However, while in some communities they stick to one of the versions of the legends, in some two or all three can be narrated. Whatever the case, these oral narrations are the only sources available for the origin of the *tsinza* since there are no other known sources, at least for now. While the first and third narrations above seemed to link the origin of the instrument to the transformation from hunter-gatherer society to a cultivation society, the second one links it to a spirit "*Cicu*". All the legends tend to "mystify" the *tsinza*. It is presented as an instrument that comes from a non-natural source and given to the Bura people.

4.4 Construction of the Tsinza – A Case Study

The two legends narrated above by Usman Boja and Audu Bata both contain some information about how the 'archetype' of the *tsinza* was constructed. While I was in Bura land to collect data for this thesis, many of the players of the instrument could not answer my questions on how the *tsinza* is constructed. According to the *tsinza* musicians I interviewed, there are experts who make the instrument, and they purchase it from them. One of such experts that the *tsinza* musicians consistently mentioned was a man named Jauro Msirawa.

Born about 58 years ago in the village of Mbulatawiwi, Jauro Msirawa is one of the few known *tsinza* constructors, and also a player in Bura land. According to him, his father, Machar Gorgum, neither played the *tsinza* nor did he know how to construct it. However, his father's elder brother and his grandfather, Koringa Dawi, were both *tsinza* players. His father bought his first *tsinza* for him when he was very young. Due to the fact that his father did not know how to play the *tsinza*, he practiced on his own and frequently visited his grandfather in the village of Shitkam, about one and half kilometers from Mbulatawiwi. According to him, he learnt how to play the *tsinza* very well and, also while he visited his grandfather, he watched how the instrument is constructed from some members of his clan in the village who were engaged in making it. Fascinated by the way the instrument was constructed, young Msirawa told himself that:

> "One day when I am old enough, I must try making the *tsinza* myself. When I was old enough, I went and cut a piece of log from *Anthlamamshi* tree. I was not sure I could handle the *Angilma* African Ebony tree, which is the one, used in making it. I cut and carved seven slabs in the shape of an older *tsinza*. I kept the slabs over the fireplace in my mothers cooking place so that the mucilage will dry out. After it has dried out, I fixed the slabs with leather thong to create the *bibethlu* (the keys tied together without the resonators). Someone heard me playing it and bought it from me. I made a second one; but these times around, a complete *tsinza*. Since then I have been making and selling the *tsinza*". (Msirawa, personal communication, 2003).

Asked whether it was that simple to make the instrument, Msirawa was quick to point out that the making of the *tsinza* is a challenge in itself, the rules of which he learnt over a period of time. After lengthy persuasion,[54] Msirawa agreed to let me observe the process of constructing the *tsinza*, but explained to me that some of the processes take a long period of time; he therefore simply described them to me.

Fig. 3.   Jauro Msirawa carving a sound plate with *nkum mara*

---

54   The construction skills are considered a secret that Msirawa only agreed to disclosed to me after he was convinced that I was interested only for scholarly purpose.

According to him, the first thing he learnt was that the tree, *angilma*,[55] used in making the *tsinza* must be felled and left to dry over a period of time in the bush. Care must be taken when cutting the tree. This he said is because "our people have this belief that some trees that want to be 'difficult' sometimes 'bleed blood.'" This apparently refers to the sap produced from some trees after it is freshly cut. The Bura interpret this as "blood" of the tree. After some time, the *tsinza* constructor goes back to the tree to check whether it has dried up. If dried, he cuts the trunk into small pieces and brings it back home. Using *nkum mara* (carving axe), each of the trunks is split and cut into the same length, but of different thicknesses, with the ends of each piece of wood bigger than the middle.

Fig. 4. Tools for *Tsinza* Construction (*nkum mara, indla deaha* and *indla*)

The bark of the wood is removed and a small, smooth pebble from a river is used to polish the pieces of wood smooth by grinding it.

Msirawa brought twenty-one pieces of wood out from his room that had already been prepared for that stage in the process. In the open space in front of his compound, he dug a rectangular hole into the ground about one and half meters wide and half a meter deep. He spread a layer of sand brought from a river into the dug hole. He then carefully arranged the twenty-one pieces of wood on the sand inside the hole, separating them so that they did not touch each other. The hole was then filled in with sand until full. Pieces of chopped wood were arranged over the hole and a fire ignited. Msirawa explained to me that the fire must be kept burning for seven days

---

55   African Ebony – *Diospyros crassiflora*.

to allow the *dumwar* (mucilage/gum) left in the body of the pieces of wood to dry out completely. The heat is also used to harden the wood.

After seven days of burning fire over the hole, it was left to cool off for five days. The sand used to cover the hole was dug out and the slabs taken out. Msirawa struck each of them with a stick as he took them out. Once he was satisfied with the slabs of wood, the next task was to obtain the seven cow horns that will serve as the resonators. This he said must be picked one after the other from seven different market days in the locality.[56] The butchers usually slaughter a cow on a market day to sell the beef. The horns of a slaughtered cow are discarded. The cow horns must never be picked from the same market and one must be careful not to pick horns from the same side of the head of a slaughtered cow. This means that if a horn is picked from the right side of a cow's head on a particular market day, the next one must be from the left. This applies until the seven horns required are collected.[57]

When asked whether this is still the practice considering that the populations of Bura villages have considerably increased over the years, several cows are slaughtered each day in almost all villages, and the cow horns can easily be collected in a short period of time, Msirawa admitted that not all *tsinza* constructors still observe this practice. He was quick to point out, though, that he still did:

"Our ways have changed... Many have abandoned our traditional indigenous practices and they are no longer afraid of the sanctions our gods will impose on them when they do certain things not according to the traditions. They have embraced new religions, foreign to our own. Their new religions allow them to do things the way they want it" (Msirawa, personal communication, 2003)

Msirawa collected the cow horns from different market days of the locality around his village. He explained to me that all cow horns consist of seven layers and to get the resonators for the *tsinza*, six must be removed. The horns are taken to a river, soaked in a pond, and left for seven days. This was to soften it so that the six unwanted layers can be easily removed.

Using a sharp carving knife, he carefully scraped to the required thickness for all the seven horns after they were brought out of the pond at the river. The sharp tips of the horns were also cut off, leaving small openings. Pieces of round calabash made from a larger broken one, with holes pierced

---

56 A particular day of a week is dedicated as market day in large Bura villages.
57 This is done apparently for the resonators to properly fit into the construction, but the constructors of the instrument try to "mystify" it. In the arrangement of the resonators, it would be difficult for cow horns from same side of the head to fit in side by side since both would be same directionally. It is, therefore, necessary to alternate them.

in the middle of it, were pushed in around the holes where the tips of the horns were cut of. *Ndivirciri* (Bee wax) was applied over it to hold it in place.

Having obtained the resonators, the next step was to carve the *Kugwa tsinza* (a curved plank) over which the resonators would be fastened. The curved plank is usually made from *nfur debiro*.[58] Unlike the *angilma* cut for making the slabs, Msirawa brought the piece of *debiro* trunk home fresh. According to him, it is a soft wood and the *kugwa tsinza* must be carved when it is still wet, otherwise the required shape will not be achieved. After carving it, a long pointed needle-shaped metal with a wooden handle, *afa*, inserted into fire until it became hot red, was used to pierce holes into it at several places. Msirawa explained that leather thong would be passed through these holes while fastening the resonators and a wooden hoop later. The *kugwa tsinza* was sent to a woman, Maravi, for decoration with traditional motifs on the back of it.

Fig. 5. Kugwa *Tsinza*

Msirawa then made a wooden hoop from the twig of a tree. This was fastened to the *kugwa tsinza*, using two of the big holes earlier pierced on the two ends. The open ends of the cow horn resonators were also fastened to the middle of the *kugwa tsinza* below the wooden slabs. The gaps between the resonators were filled with *ndivirciri* bee wax. This extends to the mouth of the resonators. It overlapped the mouth leaving it in such a way that it can be used to reduce or increase the opening. Msirawa explained that the purpose of this is to regulate the intensity of the vibrations; which in turn

---

58   Frankincense tree – *Boswellia carteri*.

depends on temperature. If it is hot, the bee wax is pushed down and when it is cold, it is opened up.

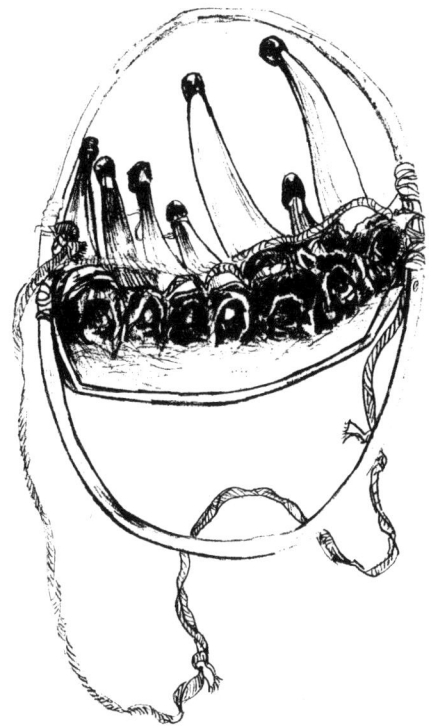

Fig. 6. Setting of resonators in the Kugwa tsinza

Satisfied with the whole frame of the *tsinza*, it was time to work on the keys. Msirawa carefully selected seven slabs out of the ones prepared earlier and laid them out on the ground in front of him. He also brought out seven slabs from an older *tsinza* and kept them beside him. One after the other, he picked a slab from the new ones laid in front of him and struck it with a single *tsinza* beater. He did the same with an older one. Using *Kum Mara*, he chopped off bits of wood from the inner side of a new slab. This was repeated for all the slabs until he got the required tone for each. He referred to this process as *nthlibila kulyang* (removing the "bad voice").

The seven keys were then fastened together with a leather thong running through the top and the bottom with an extension at each end. The extended ends of the thongs were used to suspend the keys above the resonators by tying them to the wooden hoop. At this point, Msirawa started referring to the keys by their Bura terms. He arranged them in the following order from the left hand side to the right: *anggir matsikar* (the big left), *elang mat-*

75

sikar (the small left), *kuba at kiri* (meet on me), *elang diffu* (the small middle), *anggir diffu* (the big middle), *elang mazim* (the small right) and *anggir mazim* (the big right). The key fastened together in this order is referred to as *bibethlu* (See fig. 12).

In suspending the keys over the resonators, Msirawa explained, that each one must be above the one that corresponds to its tone. The lengths of the cow horn resonators depend on the vibrations of the keys, to ensure optimal amplification of the sound. A smaller horn is placed under the key that has the higher tone while the biggest one is placed below the key with the bass tone.

Fig. 7. *Tsinza* Player

But before fixing the key to the frame of the *tsinza*, Msirawa embarked on what he considered an important and delicate aspect of constructing a *tsinza*. The cut end—orifice—of the resonators must be closed. He considers it delicate because this must be done with *titau* (membrane of cocoons from a spider). It must be located on the wall of the buildings of the compound and carefully peeled off, and it must also be treated before use. According to him, *titua* is made up of seven layers, six of which must be removed, leaving one to be used to close the orifice. He brought out some that he had removed so time ago and put them into the palm of his right hand. He took a small quantity of cold ashes from a fireplace and added them to the *titau*. He squeezed it in his palm gently over and over, checking it from time to time, until he was satisfied that six of the seven layers were gone. The very thin remainder of the *titau* was carefully laid out on a flat piece of wood and cut to sizes to cover the orifice. Each was placed on the *ndivirciri* earlier placed around the cut tips of the horns. Holding a fire-lit piece of wood some distance away from the *titau* placed on the *ndivirciri*, Msirawa gently closed the orifice on each horn. This according to him is what gives the *tsinza* the buzzing sound it produces. The keys were then suspended over the resonators by tying the loose ends of the leather thong used in binding them together.

For the *Kuli tsinza* (beaters), a pair of Y-shaped sticks were cut from selected small branches of a tree.[59] The bark was carefully removed. Msirawa explained that the *kuli tsinza* are carved to form a Y-shape so as to enable a player of the instrument to strike from one to four notes at the same time.

4.4.1 Construction and its Language

While constructing the *tsinza*, Msirawa consistently used some Bura terms to describe some of the processes. He was particular about *nthlibila kulang* (removing the very bad 'voice') from the sound plates. Throughout the construction process, he referred to the sound plates as *mji* (pl.) /*mda* (sing.) (People/person). He explained that:

> "Just as human beings have voices, so also does the *tsinza*. Some people's voices are sharp while others are deep... Some are nice while others not nice. The *tsinza* is a mixture of voices so it must be arranged in such a way that it gives *kuraku na msira* a sweet voice" (Msirawa, Personal communication, 2003).

The sound produced by each sound plate is considered as *Kuraku* (voice). Before the sound plates are given their *kuraku*, they are considered to be *wawi* (erratic; having no fixed or regular course). Each sound plate must therefore be treated carefully so as to give it the "correct" *kuraku*. This explains why in the process of fixing the keys together, Msirawa used older sound plates to determine the correct *kuraku* for each of the new ones. He further explained that:

---

59 Soft wood trees. Beaters made of *angilma* cannot be used in playing the *tsinza* because it would be too hard and cannot produce the desired sound, according to Msirawa

"*Mji* (People) talk amongst themselves... It is expected that each *mda* (person) speak in a tone that is not *wawi*. All human *Kuraku* (voices) falls under seven categories. Each of the seven sound plates represents one category. Any of the *Kuraku* that does not fall into any of the seven categories is considered to have a *kulyang* (bad voice). Such a *kulang* must therefore be removed".

Msirawa considered the removing of the *Kulang* the most important aspect in the whole process of *tsinza* construction. For him, it is what distinguishes a "good" *tsinza* from a "bad" one.

It is interesting how the tsinza maker, and indeed the Bura people more generally, attribute a human characteristic to the *tsinza* sound plates. *Kuraku*, voice, is a human characteristic. The Bura would not attribute *kuraku* to animals. The moo of a cow for example, would be referred to as *tuwa* (crying) rather than *kuraku*. So also is the baa of a sheep or bleat of a goat. The Bura personify the *tsinza* sound plates. The sound plates are referred to as *mji* people, and having *kuraku* voice. This may not be unconnected with the fact that the *tsinza* was originally a funeral instrument. It is thought to be the only instrument that is understood as having a connection with the Bura ancestral world. It facilitates "communication" between the living and the dead members of the society. The instrument "speaks", and it is only humans who can speak. Therefore, the sound plates are spoken about as "people" with "voices".

Being an instrument that is used to "communicate" with the ancestors, great effort is put in to the construction to ensure that when used, the "communication" is not *wawi*. The makers are, therefore, particular about removing *kulang* from each *kuraku*. In the Bura worldview, the ancestors must never be spoken to in a *kuraku* that is *wawi*. The ancestors play a significant role in the everyday life of a Bura, so they must be addressed in a *kuraku na msira* "sweet voice".

Bura, being a tonal language, therefore, takes the combination of the *kuraku* of the seven sound plates of the *tsinza* to produce what could be termed as *kuraku na msira*. Perhaps this was what informed Msirawa's assertion, and indeed that of the Bura, that human voices are categorized into seven. The seven categories of human voices are linked to the seven keys of the *tsinza*. However, the voices must neither be arranged in an ascending nor descending order for a *kuraku na msira*. Nonetheless, the voices that are similar to each other must be placed together as is the case in the arrangement of the keys of the *tsinza*.

Fig. 8. *Tsinza* Players

4.4.2 Decoration and its Meaning

The *tsinza* is often adorned with hanging tassels, carvings and other decorations. The hanging tassels are usually made of different colored thread. They are fastened to or suspended from the cattle horn resonators. According to Msirawa, the players do this purely for decoration and the tsinza makers themselves never do it. Some of the players insisted that it has no special meaning attached to it. Each player does it in such a way to make his instrument look distinct. Sometimes, little carvings of animal or human figures are suspended together with the hanging tassels. This too, some of the musicians insisted, has no meaning. However, some of them conceded that the carvings are sometimes protection charms against other musicians who may be envious[60] of their playing skills and cause bad luck for them. There is a belief amongst them that an envious musician could cause an instrument to not "sound right" or for something to go wrong at the peak of performance, a situation all *tsinza* players dread.

The most interesting of the decorations is the one done on the back of the *Kugwa tsinza*. The decorations on the back are formed by the use of a multiplicity of fine lines, sometimes with the interplay of figures. The technique used to achieve the decorations is pyro-engraving, whereby a red-hot, leaf-

---

60   Rivalry is generally common among Bura musicians.

shaped metal point set in a wood handle is used to burn lines into the surface of *kugwa tsinza* (Berns, 1985). Interestingly,[61] women mainly do the decoration of the *Kugwa tsinza*. In a few exceptional cases, men do them as well.

Fig. 9. *Tsinza* Decoration

Fig. 10. *Tsinza* Decoration

Traditionally, in Bura society the art of calabash decoration is the work of women. Perhaps this could be the reason why the makers of the *tsinza* ask

---

61   This is interesting because *tsinza* construction and playing is performed by men.

women calabash decorators to decorate the *kugwa tsinza*. This was the case with the one I observed being constructed by Msirawa during fieldwork. Maravi, a female master calabash decorator adorned the instrument (see fig. 5).

The decorations are mainly similar to the decoration on calabashes. It is always a combination of at least two or more decorative motifs, but one of them is conspicuous which may result in the name of the decoration. The names of some of the motifs include: *Thlambila* (basket), *Likandim* (cowries' shell), *Kucivisuda* (two buttocks), *Ncabugla* (dove's eye), *Mbwarbaka* (fish trap) and many more. The ones mentioned are most popular amongst *tsinza* musicians. Sometimes the decorations are described by a technical vocabulary describing the kind of line being made: *Shuwa*, (thick, black line), *Ntsiva* (dots), *Tankirnta* (Crosshatching), and *Bili* (curve).

There are no specific rules as to which decoration should be done on a *tsinza* when it is being constructed. Msirawa explained that sometimes the builders of the instrument make their own choice. However, the choices made by most musicians are an avenue for achieving recognition and prestige. Many are particular about their instrument being the best. Sometimes it is left to the discretion of the woman engaged to do the decoration. However, it appears that decorative motifs are passed from one generation to the other. There are similarities in the decorative motifs of older instruments[62] and newer ones though styles of the overall decoration do change. It was explained that styles had changed and that the musicians and sometimes the women decorators wanted "modern" designs. Perhaps this explains why some of the decorations on the back of some newer instruments appear less detailed than the older ones.

---

62 Older decorations of the instruments were difficulf to photograph because of faintness.

4.4.3 Organological Description of the *Tsinza*

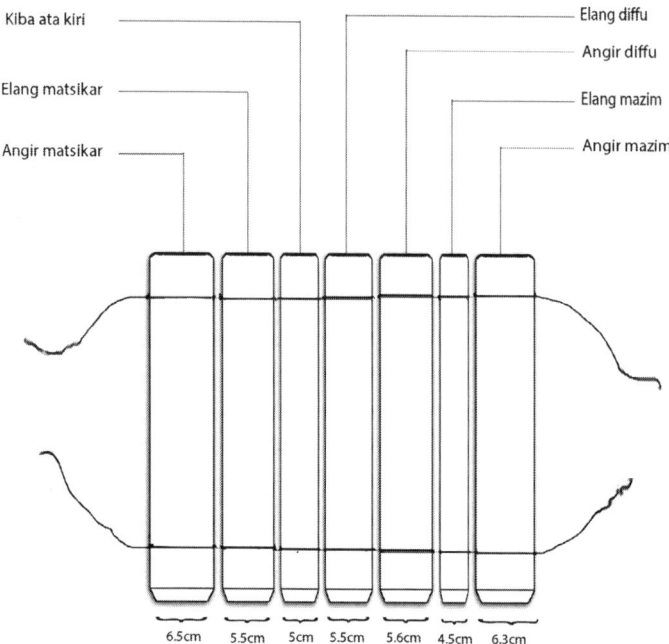

Kiba ata kiri

Elang matsikar

Angir matsikar

Elang diffu

Angir diffu

Elang mazim

Angir mazim

6.5cm 5.5cm 5cm 5.5cm 5.6cm 4.5cm 6.3cm

(the length of each slab measures 33.5cm)

Fig. 11. *Tsinza* Organology

In Bura taxonomy, the seven sounds-plates/slabs have the following names: *anggir matsikar* (the big left), *elang matsikar* (the small left), *kiba ata kiri* (meet on me), *elang diffu* (the small middle), *anggir diffu* (big middle), *elang mazim* (small right) and *anggir mazim* (big right). Apart from describing the names of the sound-plates, these terms connote other meanings in the Bura language. For example, the term *anggir* refers to a 'mature female';[63] *matsikar* refers to the left hand side or when something is not done in the 'accepted way'; *mazim* refers to the right hand side or when something is done 'correctly' as it should be done; *diffu* means center or the heart; *kuba ata* means to meet on; *kiri* means my head or on me; and *elang* means small or tiny. The use of these terms clearly demonstrates that the *tsinza* is given the attributes of a human. These same terms are also terms that are used to describe some of the parts of the human body or the daily activities that a human being engages in. When an *anggir* (mature female) speaks, for example, the voice sounds deeper (low) than that of a young or tiny person

---

63   Mainly of animals but sometimes applicable to humans for descriptive purposes.

(*elang*). There is also *anggir diffu* and *elang diffu*, *diffu* being the 'heart' or the 'centre' of a thing.

The sound plates of the *tsinza* are neither arranged in a rising nor in a falling order, but those tones are neighbouring each other that are related in the octave ratio (Vogels, 1989). Within a pentatonic, i.e. five-tonal scale on an instrument with seven keys, the octaves exist between the two lowest and two highest tones. The *tsinza* does not have its lowest key *elang diffu* to the extreme left, but rather right in the centre next to the second highest tone *anggir diffu*; and, the second lowest is arranged in the 2nd position to the right next to the highest tone *anggir mazim*. This kind of spiral order and the shape of the beaters are utilized by players to perform in octaves, that is, exclusively playing octave tones together. The musicians categorically declared it impossible to play different intervals as in, for instance, the second highest and the second lowest tones at the same time. The musical aim of such a construction would be to put melo-rhythmic accents in order to set melodic emphasis as well, apart from rhythmic stress (Vogels 1989). This arrangement is certainly one of the factors that make the *tsinza* unique in the African context.

4.4.4 Regional Differences in Construction and Decoration

While conducting fieldwork, I have often heard of musicians referring to differences between the *tsinza* of one Bura region and another. Bura land is divided into South, East and West Bura.[64] Msirawa, whom I observed construct a *tsinza*, was of a similar view. According to him, there are regional differences in the construction of the instrument.

The Bura who live in the western area of Bura land, where Msirawa comes from, consider both their *tsinza* playing skills and construction superior to that of the Bura who live in the southern area. Msirawa belongs to the Nganjiwa clan who considered itself as having the exclusive prerogative of making and playing the *tsinza*. Those from this clan are the dominant *tsinza* musicians in Bura land; and they refer to the *tsinza* made from the southern area as *tsinza mya Hawul* (*tsinza* of the Hawul Valley) or sometimes with a derogatory term *hahyipu kugwa* (broken calabash). For them, the music produced by such a *tsinza* is like the sound produced by a cracked calabash when struck. The sound produced by a cracked calabash is unpleasant to a Bura, thereby, the derogatory term *"hahyipu Kugwa."* The Nganjiwa clan members pride themselves on being the inventors[65] of the *tsinza*. They, therefore, see constructing and playing the instrument as their

---

64   Based on directional location of villages.
65   The claim is based on the legends about the instrument.

special preserve. They believe that any *tsinza* that is not made by someone from their clan cannot produce "good" music.

The Bura living in the southern part of Bura land, on the other hand refer to those who live in the west as *Hina*. According to them, many of the people who are predominantly living in the West of the area are not Bura. They are, therefore, of the view that the music of the *tsinza* played by these people is not in the Bura language. It is rather in the *Hina* language. For them, this is the major difference between their *tsinza* and that of the people who live in the West of the area.

As for the decoration of the instrument, the people in the West see their decorations as better than those in the South. The motifs used are the same. However, the decorations on the instruments constructed in the South tend to be more of a simplified version in its execution compared with the ones from the West.

Despite what the people from the two regions see as differences in their *tsinza,* a close look at the instrument from *"mya Hawul"* or the one from the *"Hina"* shows that they are the same. What the two groups see as regional difference in their instruments could perhaps best be explained in terms of the skills of craftsmanship in the construction and decoration. While the builders of the instrument from West Bura land still insist on using indigenous traditional materials required for its construction, those in the southern part appear not to pay much attention to it. For example, the most ideal tree for the production of the sound plates is the *angilma* tree. Those in the South do not really insist on this. Instead they use *anthlimamshi.*[66] According to Msirawa, *anthlimamshi* contains too much sap so it would never dry out properly to produce a "good sound".

Also, instead of using *ndivirciri* mixed to close the gaps between the resonators, the Bura in the South sometimes use bitumen.[67] Closing the gaps between the resonators is very important in the construction of the instrument. *Ndivirciri* is not only important for closing the gaps, but it also extends to the mouth of the resonators and this is very important in controlling the intensity of the vibrations. If it is very hot and a large mass of sound flows into the horn, the opening has to be narrowed, whereas if it is cold it has to be widened. Unlike *ndivirciri,* when exposed to heat, bitumen can easily melt. It is, therefore, difficult to achieve the aspect of narrowing or closing the gaps if filled by bitumen. The sound produced by such a *tsinza* would not be the same as the one that is used for *ndivirciri.* Again, instead of using a leather thong for fastening the *tsinza,* plastic strings are used in the construction of the instrument in the South of the area.

---

66   African rosewood
67   The Bura first came into contact with bitumen in the early 1970s when tarred road construction started in the area.

Perhaps the changes in the materials used in the construction of the *tsinza* in the South could be attributed to modern influences. Bitumen and plastic strings are modern to indigenous Bura culture. Christianity came into Bura land from the southern part of the area before spreading to the other parts. Many in the South converted to the new religion while many in the West of the area did not. Those who converted to Christianity were taught to abandon many of their indigenous practices. Perhaps this explains why the constructors of the instrument in southern parts of the area could readily accept "modern" materials in constructing the *tsinza*, more so than those in the West.

4.4 Conclusion

The information presented in this chapter is an attempt at offering a history of the *tsinza* and providing a description of its construction techniques. The chapter draws heavily from oral history since our knowledge of the instrument is limited, as no literature exists on Bura music. However, literature on xylophones in Africa with a similar order of keys provides valuable information that can assist in the interpretation of oral history and the construction technique of the Bura *tsinza*. The legends about the origin of the instrument and the information on the construction of the instrument demonstrate that it is closely associated with Bura identity. Having discussed the *tsinza* in the context of other African xylophones and its oral history and construction, I now turn in the next chapter to other Bura musical instruments and the linguistic approach to describing them.

5 A Linguistic Approach to the Description of Bura Musical Instruments

5.1 Introduction

This chapter discusses Bura musical instruments more generally, focusing on words or terminology used in describing them and the different ways of playing them. However, this is done with the goal of understanding whether there is a relationship between the terminologies used to describe other Bura musical instruments and the language used in the construction of the *tsinza* as detailed in the preceding chapter.[68] The terminology used by a culture primarily reflects that culture's interest and concerns (i.e., worldview). The power of language to reflect culture and thinking was first proposed by American linguist and anthropologist, Edward Sapir and his student Benjamin Whorf. The Sapir-Whorf hypothesis (as cited in Peoples and Alan, 1991) states:

> [Language] powerfully conditions all our thinking about social problems and processes. Human beings do not live in the objective world alone, nor alone in the world of social activity as ordinarily understood but are very much at the mercy of the particular language which has become the medium of expression for their society... The fact of the matter is that the "real world" is to a large extent unconsciously built up on language habits of the group... The worlds in which different societies live are distinct worlds, not merely the same world with different labels attached. (Sapir 1964: 68-69)

With this hypothesis, "Sapir and Whorf believe that language helps define the worldview of its speakers. It does so, in part, by providing labels for certain kinds of phenomena (things, concepts, qualities, and actions), which different languages define according to different criteria" (Peoples and Alan 1991:62). Bura terms used in describing musical instruments and the way they are played will be explored to determine aspects of their worldview that might be embedded in the language generally used to discuss music. The discussion of the instruments is based on Hornbostel and Sach's (1961) classification of musical instruments.

---

68 cf. Chapter 4.

5.2 Drums and their Ways of Beating – Sur tsayeri na fit fitari ka kisim (Membranophones)

Different types of drums exist in Bura society. The common name for drums is *ganga*.[69] Musical ensembles that use *ganga* employ two types of drums: the big drum—*ganga*; and a small one—*kwala*. Apart from these two drums is a third one, *dlimbwal*, that is strictly a ritual drum and not used in any ensemble.

5.2.1 Ganga

This is a barrel-shaped drum with *kisim* (skin/membrane) covering both ends of the barrel. The *kisim* is held in place by *dzir* (snare) tension chords. It is beaten with a curved stick *kuli ganga* and the hands (See fig 12). *Dzir* refers to a thin but very strong chord traditionally braided out of leather or, in modern times, out of industrial materials like synthetic polymer. The Bura consider such a chord to be tough and not easy to cut. Anything tied with it, therefore, remains firm and does not easily break. The word *dzir* is sometimes used in everyday language to illustrate how firm or tough something needs to be tied. For example, in building a compound fence, which is constructed out of cornstalks[70] tied to wooden poles fixed in the ground, the builders may be directed to afix it tight "*apa mbwa dzir ganga*" (literarily translated as "tying it tight like the tension chords of a drum). If in the process of pulling to make it tight the rope breaks, the individual who happens to be caught in such a situation may also be questioned about why he pulled it too hard, as if he were handling *dzir ganga*. Here the language used in tuning a *ganga* is also used in the construction of a compound fence. This is an indication of the interplay of words taken from the vocabulary of dealing with the tuning of a musical instrument. Both are dealing with one word *dzir* yet symbolically convey different meanings. One meaning is a request to do the act of tying well, by pulling as if "tuning" a *ganga;* and the other is that of "over pulling" it and making the "tuning" out of order.

Similarly, the word *kuli* is also used to describe the various wooden handles of farm and some household implements. The handle of hoes, sickles, knives and diggers are referred to as *kuli* (e.g. *kuli mindziha* a hoe handle, *kuli thlahu* a sickle handle, etc.). A stout, heavy stick is also called *kuli*. Though, when the word *kuli* is mentioned in every day language, the immediate image that comes to the mind is that of a "stout heavy stick" that can

---

69 Common name for drums across Northern Nigeria.
70 Stalks of sorghum.

be used in different contexts, especially as a weapon to strike an enemy, to separate sorghum or corn from the cob, and so on. The curved drumstick, though small in size, is used to strike the *ganga* to produce a loud sound. It is, therefore, considered as accomplishing a similar task to *"kuli"* (a stout heavy stick). In this case it is the output of sound produced by striking the drum membrane *kisim* that qualifies the little drumstick as a *kuli*. *Kuli* is required to "beat" the *ganga* to produce sound.

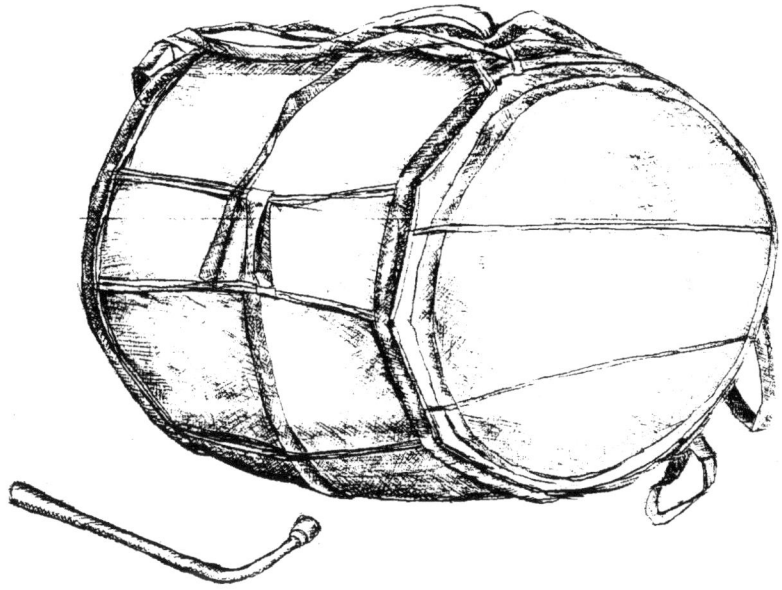

Fig. 12. *Ganga*

5.2.2 *Kwala*

The *Kwala* is a small hourglass shaped drum with a single membrane and tension chords *dzir* attached. It is suspended around the neck on a leather thong and beaten with two short flexible beaters made out of textile material held in both hands. It is beaten in a repetitive regular rhythmic motion *dzakwaraku* with a high-pitched tone *nyararau* (See fig. 13). Although the words *dzakwaraku* and *nyararau* are used in the "language" of playing the *kwala*, both words are also used in everyday language. *Dzakwaraku*, for example, is used to describe something that is uneven, rough, or not smooth in shape. A thatch roofing[71] of a house that is not properly

---

71 House roofs in Bura villages were made out of thatched grass before the introduction of modern roofing materials.

laid would be described as *dzakwaraku*. It is a term that can be used to describe a regular motion and something that is irregular as well. The sustained rhythmic tone of the *kwala* for the Bura is *dzakwaraku* while the "rough" thatching of a house could also be described as *dzakwaraku*. Indeed, anything that has a rough finish is described in this manner. *Nyararau*, though mostly associated with noise, can also be used as an expression to indicate that something is "sharp". Too much salt *una* in food, for example, can be said to be *una nyararau*; so, too, is the sharp blade of a knife—*indla tsiltsila nyararau*.

Fig. 13. *Kwala*

Apart from the two drums described above, there is a special Bura drum used only during funerals and for sending "signals"[72] in cases of emergency. This drum is called *dlimbwal*. It is a kettledrum played with the bare palms of both hands (see Fig. 14).

---

72   To alert of impending danger.

Fig. 14. Dlimbwal

Each of these *ganga* are tuned at various pitches. However, there are no single words to describe whether a *ganga* is loud, fast etc. Rather, the action is described. When a *ganga* is beaten loud, it is described as:

ganga ni a tuwa

The word *"tuwa"* means, "crying". Crying is something that has to do with emotions. A sad person or someone who is severely injured might cry because of pain. But the bleats of a sheep, the moo of a cow or the twitter of birds are also all considered by the Bura to be "cries". Likewise, the sound or melody produced by beating the *ganga* is referred to as a "cry". Therefore, the Bura term *"tuwa"* not only refers to crying that involves the physical shedding of tears when in pain or an emotional state that makes one cry, but also to melody or sound produced by musical instruments or animals.

The Bura describe the manner in which a *ganga* is played in different ways. The description is determined by the *"tuwa"* it produces. When it is played fast, it is described as:

ganga ni taktartaktar dzau
taktartaktar means: too fast.

When it is played softly or gently, it is described as:

ndigirndigira: meaning to pull, to draw.

The word *ndigira* also means to lead. Someone who walks at the head of a group of travellers, for example, on a journey, is considered as *mdir ndigira laku* (translated as one who "pulls" the road.)
When it is played energetically, it is described as:

tsá duna dzau = energetic beating
tsá = hit, strike, beat
duna = energy, power, strength

When it is played unmusically or incorrectly, it is described as:

tsá daka daka

When it is played with a high-pitched tone, it is described as:

tuwa ganga ni nyararau

This literarily translates as, 'the "crying" of the drum is sharp'.
When it is played with low-pitched tone, it is described as:

ganga ni adi akwa tuwa wa

This translates as, 'the drum is not "crying" loud'.
Though the Bura term *daka* is used to describe incorrect drumming, it is also used in every day language to describe other actions or situations. The action of someone who does something "ignorantly" is considered *dakakur.* A speech that is not delivered very well could be described as *gari* (talk/ speech) *daka daka,* so too is any public event that is not properly carried out according to the expectation of the members of the society. The action of the organizers of such an event would be described as *daka daka.*

5.2.3 Words Describing or Naming Musical Ensembles with only Drum Instruments

The Bura people have no musical ensemble that only contains drums. The drum is played with other instruments as an accompaniment (e.g. *tsinza* and *Algaita*). However, drummers are referred to as *kidá* (sing.) *kidáyeri* (pl.). A drummer is thus addressed with the word *kida* as a title (e.g. *kida* Bukar Bishi). The word "*kida*" has other meanings in Bura language as well:

kidá = to beg/begging, to appeal to, to beseech
kìda = Bamboo – material commonly used by the Bura in house roofing
kidā = thigh of a human being or any animal

The Bura use the word *kidá* (beg/begging) in different ways. The term is used to show apprehension to a person who is lazy and relies on begging from other members of the society in order to survive. Such a person is considered "weak" and always looked down upon, but might sometimes receive material or monetary gifts from other members of the society who have the means to assist. Such a person's attitude is considered negative. Musicians are also considered as *mjir kidá*, beggars of a sort. Though in this case, they use their music to earn small sums. They sing people's praises, and in return receive material or monetary reward from them. What they do is also considered kidá (begging) but it is seen in a different, perhaps slightly more positive, light from those who seem to put effort into not working hard to earn a living, but to sustain themselves by begging.

While the term *kidá* in Bura taxonomy is derogatory, its application when it comes to musicians appears to be seen from a different perspective. In the case of *kidáyeri* (drummers) and indeed musicians generally, they make music and in the process use *ndir msira* (sweet words) to praise their patrons. It is the praises they sing with *ndir msira* that "appeals" to the "conscience" of the patrons to receive monetary rewards from them. As such, their form of *kidá* seems "acceptable" to the Bura and is not looked down upon. This might be the case because they are considered to be performing a role that society expects—fulfilling the entertainment and other needs of the people. Apart from entertainment, they sometimes serve as the means through which people can express their anger against one another or happenings in the community. Musicians in Bura society are most often not taken seriously by the people, so it is quite easy for them to serve as a mouthpiece that points out issues that do not conform to the belief and value systems of the culture. Things that they say in their music may sound like a joke, but underneath it might be a message that people understand. They are, therefore, sometimes used in expressing the pains of their patrons, since what they sing may not be challenged due to the fact that they always have a way of putting across a message without specifically referring to a person. The intended receiver might understand such a message, but he or she cannot challenge it since it came from a musician that mentions no one by name. So, whether they sing the praise of an individual or they try to get a message across, they use *ndir msira* to achieve that.

For the Bura, *ndir msira* used by musicians in praising people in their music is interpreted as *mya kidá* (language of begging). In such a "language", the musicians try to articulate the importance of a person by narrating things that might not be totally true about him, but that the person for whom it is meant appreciates. Many of the things said might be exaggerated, but acceptable within the context of social events where music making takes place.

If one takes the Bura drum music, for example, it is not praise music in the real sense of the word, which is produced on "talking drums".[73] However, when playing *bansuwe* dance music drummers add drummed phrases, which can be understood as names by the dancers, i.e. "Alhaji Dauda", "Mada Garkida," etc. It is such phrases that are considered *mya kidá* (the language of begging) and what the patrons of the drummers appreciate and respond to. Individuals or groups (e.g. a clan, village etc.) always feel elated to be "praised" at dance occasions and always respond by giving monetary rewards to the drummer.

The term *"kidá"* is, however, not used as a title when addressing Bura musicians that play other instruments. Even though they also use *mya kidá*, they are not addressed as *kidá*. The word, therefore, is only applicable to drummers and, mainly is only the lead drummer in the *bansuwe* ensemble addressed as such. A *yakandi* (lute) player, for example, is referred to as *mdir tsá Yakandi* (someone who plays the *yakandi*) and not as *kidá*.

Drummers can also be described as *"mjir (pl) tsá ganga"*, meaning drum players or *mdir (sing.) tsá ganga:* The word *"tsá"* means to hit, strike, or kick. Thus, the act of drumming is described as "beating" or "striking" the instrument. The word *"tsá"* is also used to describe the action of weaving – *tsá poa* - weaving cotton. A weaver is, therefore, referred to as *"mdir tsá poa,"* literary meaning, 'person who weaves cotton'. The Bura traditionally use the horizontal loom *kiwa*. The sound produced by the movement of the shuttle *shar tsá poa* and the "beating" of weft threads to create tension is what is described as tsá *poa*. For the Bura, the action of weaving sounds musical to the ear and is similar to drumming. The action is, therefore, described as *tsá* "beating" as well.

The word, *"tsã"* is used in another sense when referring to a third person singular - she/he. For example, *tsã ata si* means "He will come".

---

73 Hourglass-shaped drum from West Africa, whose pitch can be regulated to mimic the the tone of human speech.

5.2.4 Words Describing or Naming Musical Ensembles with Drum Instruments and any Other Instrument

Musical ensembles comprising of drummers and other instrument players are referred to as *bansuwe* groups. This group comprises of a master drummer, two to three *kwala* players, one or more *tsinza* players, an *algaita* player and a *shola* player. It is no longer common to find an ensemble comprising of all these instruments performing together in Bura land of recent. *Algaita*[74] in particular is not an indigenous Bura musical instrument. However, it is sometimes used in *bansuwe* ensemble when a player is available. The most common formation in the present time is a group comprising of a master drummer, one or two *Kwala* players, and one or two *tsinza* players as well. Such a group performs at wedding ceremonies, funerals and any Bura occasion that requires music.

5.2.5 Words Describing or Naming Musical Ensembles with Drum Instruments and Singing

There are no musical ensembles as such with only drums and singing. However, the closest to such an ensemble is the *Bansuwe* group that comprises of drums, xylophone and sometimes the *algaita*. *Bansuwe* dance is normally accompanied with singing. The *tsinza* player leads the songs, which is normally in the form of call and response. When a group includes an *algaita* player, he leads the songs and the dancers in singing after what he plays on his instrument. Sometimes one of the dancers also leads in singing. Songs usually reflect the occasion for which a dance is performed: but other songs not connected with the occasion can be brought in occasionally as well. It could, for example, be a song to praise the 'bravery' of an individual or a song of mock for the 'misdeed' of an individual. One example of a praise song is the one sung in praise of Bukar Bishi, a master drummer in Bura land. The song goes:

1. Iye... Iye... Bukar Bishi tira abwa ni ya madankyeri girai?
    Oh... oh... Did Bukar Bishi pass this way oh you young ones?
2. Ga anta hara mutu Bukar Bishi
    You behave, as someone possessed by the spirit of witchcraft because of the manner you play on the drum

---

74   More common among the Hausa and Kanuri of Northern Nigeria.

3. Ga ana geli ka ganga. Ganga nga a sha ya
   You perform so well on the drum that your style of drumming cannot be
   mistaken for another.

A mocking song can be sung during a dance occasion to mock an individual who 'misbehaves' (e.g. stealing) in the society. When this occurs, those who are good in composing songs, *thla ha* (the word *ha* means song and *thla* means to cut), create one to be sung at the next dance occasion. One who composes a song is thus referred to as *mdir thla ha*. Such people are seen as experts in selecting words that can be used in songs to convey a message without directly referring to an individual; they do not mention people by name, but yet when listened to, members of the society can make out whom or what the song is about. Such songs are usually motivated by events in the community and can sometimes happen spontaneously.

The purpose of such songs is to publicly disgrace someone who is caught, for example, stealing or doing something else considered dishonorable by society. Apart from disgracing a person who engages in such behaviours, the songs are also expected to serve as a deterrent to those that intend to engage in activities that the society frowns upon. A public disgrace of this nature is abhorred amongst the Bura.

An example of such a song is one about a man who stole a pot of soup. The story goes that a certain woman bought fresh fish—a delicacy among the Bura—and cooked it. While preparing the guinea corn mush to eat with the cooked fresh fish soup, a certain man in her neighborhood sneaked into her compound and stole her pot of soup. He took it and hid under the leaves of pumpkin plant on a pumpkin farm[75] outside the woman's compound and ate the whole soup. Unbeknownst to the fish soup thief, someone in the neighborhood witnessed him hiding under the cover of the pumpkin leaves and eating the fresh fish soup. When the woman could not find her pot of soup she raised the alarm, and the man that saw the 'soup thief' immediately disclosed to her what he had seen. The incident became known in the community and at the next dance occasion in the village, a mocking song was sung to accompany the dance. The song goes:

1. Ta nga ya Madika?
   Is it your turn to cook Madika?
2. Ta nga ya Madawi
   Is it your turn to cook Madawi?
3. Ntula si ka macikil
   The neighbour came with macikil (mush cooked and left overnight)

---

75 Pumpkin is usually grown in the open fields inbetween compounds in Bura villages.

4. Ngwalahu ku ra pi akwa thlali Hwamdla
    The monitor lizard has gone to sleep under the pumpkin leaves.

The character of the 'pot of soup thief' is compared to that of the monitor lizard,[76] which in the Bura worldview is considered a "foolish" creature. The Bura believe that the "foolishness" of a monitor lizard is displayed when it is being hunted. The creature tries to run and hide. However, it hides only by shielding its face from its attacker by taking a position behind any thick bush or protruding object, leaving its long body uncovered. Once it does not have eye contact with the hunter, it assumes that it is safe. Being a creature with a long body, it is usually difficult to hide completely. With the body exposed it is easily seen and killed by the hunter. It is this behavior that the Bura find foolish. So, by stealing a pot of soup and hiding under pumpkin leaves in the same neighbourhood in which the act was committed, the character of the pot of soup thief is comparable to a monitor lizard that tries to hide from a hunter. The pumpkin foliage is big and might appear thick yet soft, and once trampled underfoot, it collapses. Such a place could not provide a good cover to shield the thief from being seen by other neighbours. Consequently, he was caught and the above song *ha* was composed. Since the members of the community knew about the incidence, the song would be understood as mocking the character of the pot of soup thief; thus, simultaneously disgracing him and a deterring others from stealing.

5.2.6 Words Describing or Naming Musical Ensembles with Singing Only

There are no musical ensembles which solely perform acapella singing in Bura society. However, there are certain occasions where songs could be sung without any musical instruments. Occasions that could require singing in this manner include children's games (*huhura madankyar*), and some rites at funeral and rainmaking ceremonies. An example of a children's game that requires singing alone is *Kathladzi*, a popular game among young female children, especially teenagers. In the game, those taking part form a semi-circle. While singing call-and-response songs, one participant after another, dances forward from the rest of the group, and swiftly moves backwards, flinging herself into the waiting hands of the others, who in turn lift her high up into the air. As soon as she lands, she falls back into the semi-circle to take part in "lifting" the next participant.

---

76   The common name for several large lizard species.

The participants in the game sing in order to praise one another, sometimes also mocking boys and girls whose behaviours are considered not to be in conformity with the way a boy or a girl should behave in the society. There are expected roles for men and women in the society and each person is expected to stick to such roles. Anything outside the "expected" behavior is considered "abnormal". There are also certain acts that become strange if done by girls and women in particular. It is, for example, considered strange when a girl or a woman steals because in the people's worldview, stealing is associated with boys and men.

Girls who steal or become mothers before marriage could become the subjects of the song teenage women sing when they play. But more often, they sing songs about teenage men with whom they have had an encounter. To provide an example, here is a mock song about a boy who is considered to be too proud of everything he does:

1. Bzir dakwi ya
    Oh young man...
2. Ga ata yanga ali wa
    Don't show me you are proud
3. Bzir dakwi huhur kuta, dekandang kir
    Young man with big stomach and small head
4. Ga ata yanga ali wa
    Don't show me you are proud
5. Ma ga ata yanga ali ma
    If you will display your pride for me
6. Iya ata yanga ala ga
    I will display my own pride for you
7. Ma ga ata yanga sule
    If you are proud of ten kobo
8. Iya ata yanga Naira
    I am proud of a Naira
9. Bzir dakwi bupcir kir
    Young man with a big head
10. Ga ata yanga ali wa
    Don't show you are proud

Another example of singing without instruments occurs at the funerals of elderly persons, where the eldest daughter of the deceased is expected to sing a dirge, especially in honor of a deceased father or mother. Such a dirge is always a reflection of the character of the deceased person. It could be sung purely to praise the good qualities of a deceased or to prove his or her innocence as a result of not having been involved in any form of witchcraft, which is a common accusation among the Bura. For example, if the rainy season does not start at the expected time, it is believed that witches have bewitched the season. Similarly, if the crop fails, it is also believed that someone has bewitched the fields. People whose parents, brothers or sisters, or even relatives are suspected of being witches are always anxious to become "free" from such accusations. One way of proving a deceased loved one's innocence from such accusation is to have the corpse kept for a long period (2-3 days) after death. This time is considered long enough for a cadaver to bloat and bleed through the mouth, nose and ears. If the cadaver does not bloat and bleed by the time it is publicly displayed, it is a proof of innocence and it is the accusers, therefore, who feel ashamed. Consequently, the eldest daughter of a deceased expresses the anxiety, fear and dilemma of the relatives by singing an elegy. The following is a dirge sung during one of such instances:

1. Ga lihar Mubi ka ra tsila indla mutur nga ni ya?
   Did you travel to Mubi for the sharpening of your witchcraft knife?
2. Ai yar na
   Oh my father
3. Da pila ga an pawa, pawa mutu
   They said you are the butcher, butcher for witches
4. Ka ra pi ambwa baba, ka ra pi ambwa
   Lay and spend the night in the room father, lay in the room
5. Ka da wuta jirir nga ni
   Let them see your innocence
6. Da pila ga pawa ngwa
   They alleged you are a butcher
7. Baba ra gai
   Oh you father
8. Pawa... pawa mutu
   Butcher... butcher for witches.

Similarly, songs for rainmaking ceremonies are usually sung without the accompaniment of "normal" musical instruments. Rainmaking ceremonies are undertaken whenever a rainy season is delayed—end of April to mid-May in most parts of Bura land—or when the season starts on time but the rains somehow stop and the crops start withering. At such occasions, children march through a village at night singing different songs invoking *Hyel* (God) to send down the rains while adults pay attention to the ritual aspects of the sacrifices. Household items, such as a calabash, are the only "instrument" used during the rainmaking ritual. The children carry them as they sing and march around the village, striking the calabashes intermittently. Conventional musical instruments are not used because such a period is not considered a period of merriment, but one for appeasing *Hyel* to send down the rains so that food, which is vital to the survival of the people, will grow. One of the songs for such occasion goes:

1. *Hyel ni ku ta*
   The clouds have gathered
2. *Su adi na mbil wa*
   Nothing remains
3. *Oh ... oh Hyel ra gai*
   Oh ... you God
4. *Ni ali yimi baba, ni ali yimi ka yeru sa*
   Give me water father; give me water so that we can drink
5. *Oh ... oh Hyel ra gai*
   Oh... you God

5.3 Suryeri ar Mbura ka Mya (Aerophones)

There are four instruments that fall under the category of aerophones in Bura land. These are: *shola* (flute), *algaita* (oboe), *timbul* (horn), *hyika* (a flute type mainly played by children).

5.3.1 Shola

The *shola* is an open, single end-blown flute with four finger holes. It is made out of guinea corn stalk. It used to be part of a Bura drum ensemble up until the early 1970s, but it no longer exists (see fig. 15).

5.3.2 *Algaita*

This is an oboe with a conical bore and three finger holes. Although the *Algaita* is not an indigenous Bura instrument, it has been present in Bura musical tradition for quite a while, and was particularly popular in the 1970s. It is normally part of the drum ensemble. It is, however, used less and less. This is because there are only a few *algaita* players around. The few that are around are mostly part of the personal band ensembles of the various traditional rulers (such as emir, district heads). This restricts their use in performance for the public. (See fig. 16)

Fig. 15. *Shola* player

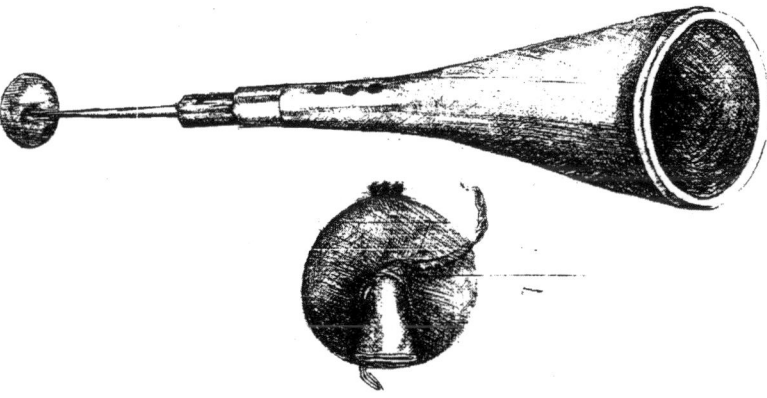

Fig. 16. *Algaita*

5.3.3 Timbul

This is an instrument made out of animal horn (mostly antelope) with the inner softer content completely removed and the pointed tip cut off (see fig. 17). The instrument is blown from the side and used for communication purposes. It is blown to announce the death of an old person, to summon people in case of emergencies (e.g. outbreak of fire, war, etc.), and to announce hunting expeditions as well. Depending on the phrases the player "speaks" on the instrument, the members of the society understand the message and respond appropriately. To announce a fire outbreak in a community, for example, what the player blows on the *timbul* is understood as *"u'u at ki"* (a house has caught fire); *u'u* meaning fire and *ki*, a house.

Fig. 17. *Timbul* player

5.3.4 Hyika

This is also an instrument made out of guinea corn stalk. A fresh piece of corn stalk is cut and the soft tissue inside carefully removed. A narrow rectangular slit is made at one end and the piece cut is carefully lifted, but not detached from the instrument. A tiny piece of twine is put around and over the slit. The twine is held tight when the instrument is being blown with the mouth. Circular breathing[77] is employed for blowing the instrument. The player closes and opens the opened end of the *hyika* with his palms to produce the melody. The Bura describes the action of blowing the instrument as *mburu mburwa ka sat sata*. *Mburu mburwa* meaning blowing in while *sat sata* means to draw out.[78]

The *hyika* is not used in any Bura musical event, but children usually use it as a solo instrument. It is, however, strictly played at a particular season of the year, when the guinea corn is ripening and peanut farms are ready for harvest. (See fig. 18)

Fig. 18. *Hyika*

5.3.5 Words Describing or Naming Musical Ensembles With Aerophones

The Bura would describe the *algaita* player as *mdir mbur algaita* (someone who "blows" the *algaita*) and the *timbul* player as *mdir mbur timbul* (someone who "blows" the *timbul*). Similarly, a *shola* player would be described as *mdir mbur shola* (someone who "blows" the *shola*). There are no single Bura words to describe these categories of musicians.

The Bura people do not have musical ensembles consisting only of aerophones. However, the *timbul* (an animal horn) as described earlier is used to announce the death of an old person and emergencies such as a sudden attack by enemies, fire outbreak and so on. Similarly, there are no musical ensembles that only play the *algaita* or *shola*.

---

77 Technique used by players of some wind instruments to produce continous tone without interuption.
78 In this case the human breath.

5.3.6 Words Describing or Naming Musical Ensembles with Aerophones and any Other Musical Instrument

There is no special name for musical ensembles with aerophones with the accompaniment of any other instrument. By contrast, a *bansuwe* group refers to an ensemble with drums combined with any other instrument. The Bura term that would describe an ensemble including aerophones and other instruments such as drums, would be *mjir sur mburmbura ka sur tsátsáyeri*, or people who play instruments that are 'blown' and 'beaten'. Bura aerophone instruments are seldom played solo. They are usually used as an accompaniment to the *bansuwe* ensemble.

5.4. Sur Tsayeri ka Nvada na Kula Fita (Idiophones)

The category of idiophone comprises the *tsinza* (xylophone), *Bara* (rattles), *kace – kace* (rattles), *humbutu* (clay pot), and *kugwa* (calabash). For information on the *tsinza* see Chapter 4 of this thesis.

5.4.1 Bara

These are two pairs of ankle rattles worn by men during *waksha-waksha* dance to produce a jingling sound (*grip kengkeng*) to match the ongoing tunes played on the *ganga* and *tsinza* (see fig. 19). It is not a musical instrument that is played per se, but the sound produced by the rhythmic movement of the dancers adds to the percussion setup.

Fig. 19. *Bara*

5.4.2 Kace – Kace

The *kace-kace* is another form of rattle. It is made out of small pieces of broken calabashes cut into a round shape with a small hole made in the middle of each. A number of these pieces of broken calabashes cut into shapes are arranged on a tiny, but hard stick. The small stick is passed through the tiny hole made on each of the broken calabashes and are left to move freely on it. The finished *kace-kace* is then shaken with the two hands to produce a rhythmic sound. (See fig. 20).

Fig. 20. Kace–Kace Players

5.4.3 Humbutu

The *humbutu* is a small clay pot instrument. The open mouth of the pot is placed on the bare stomach of the player and he holds it with one hand and strikes it with the other, lifting open one side of the mouth of the pot at intervals to produce a melody. Rattles made from a broken calabash are used as accompaniment (See figs. 21 and 22).

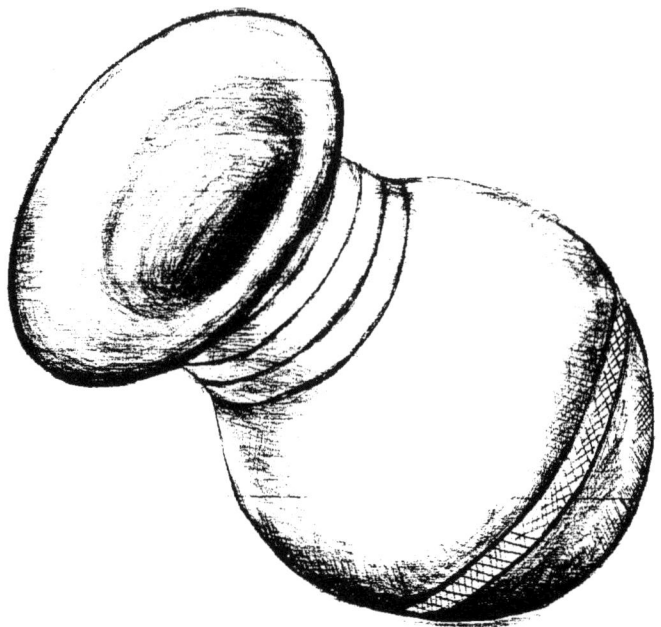

Fig. 21. *Humbutu*

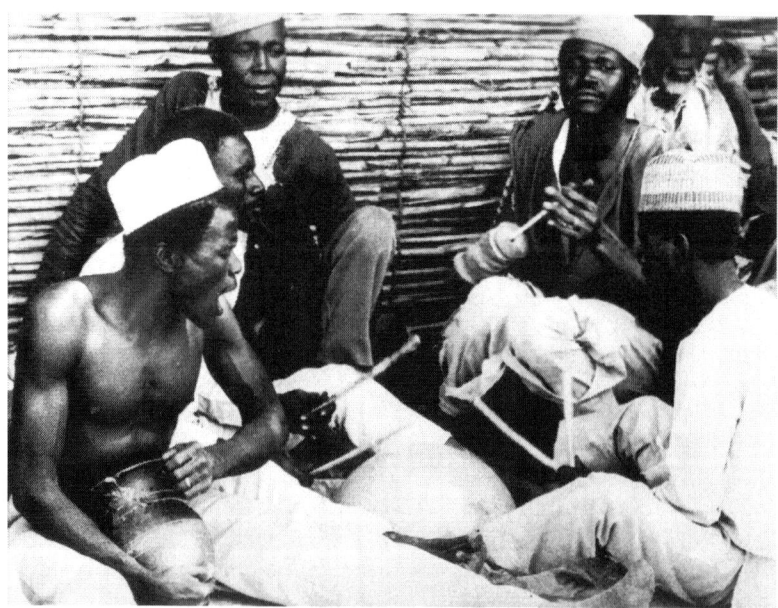

Fig. 22. Alhassan Saltuwa and group performing *Humbutu* music.

5.4.4 *Kugwa*

This instrument is made out of calabash gourd cut into two halves. The open end of the instrument is placed on the ground and two players beat it with two small sticks each (see Fig. 24). It is used as an accompaniment to the *humbutu* and in a few cases to the *tsinza* music performed at wedding ceremonies. The use of the instrument as accompaniment at events, wedding ceremonies in particular, is a recent development in the area.

Fig. 23. *Kugwa* players

5.5 Sur Tsayeri na ka Mpila Fit Fita ka Suwur Puwa (Chordophones)

Chordophones are string instruments that are played by plucking. Bura instruments that fall under this category include the *gulum* and *yakandi*.

5.5.1 Gulum

Fig. 24. *Gulum* player

The *gulum* is a long-necked spike lute with a resonator composed of a leather-covered gourd (*mpila fitfita*). It is three stringed and usually accompanies the praise singer. One of the strings (*suwur puwa*) is shorter than the other two, but all are fastened on a long stick (*wuliya gulum*) that passes through the resonating chamber. Plucking (*tsá*) the strings with the fingers produces the sound. The player wears a brass bracelet (*liya tsi*) on the hand he uses in playing the instrument from time to time to produce a sound that compliments the melody. The instrument player sits on the ground (*at adi*) or on a short stool (*kulahu*). The *gulum* is used as a solo instrument mainly, but more recently a few of its players are accompanied by *kugwa* players (See fig. 24). A player of the instrument is referred to as *deaha gulum; deaha* being the Bura word for a clever person, an expert. A person who is considered an expert in his profession is referred to as *deaha*; a blacksmith would be addressed as *deaha bdla,* and so on. It appears, however, that the use of the word in relation to music pertains to the *gulum* player. The Bura I worked with could not explain why this is, but it may not be unconnected to the role an instrumentalist plays in the rites associated with the separation of twins, triplets or quadruplets from the "spirit world." The rite is called *lita zibil* and *gulum* music is an essential part of it.[79]

5.5.2 Yakandi

The *yakandi* is a short-necked spike lute. It is two-stringed and like the *gulum,* usually accompanies the praise singer as well. It has a calabash resonator that is smaller than that of the *gulum.* Again, plucking the strings with the fingers produces sound. In rare cases, its players are also called *deaha yakandi.* (See fig. 25)

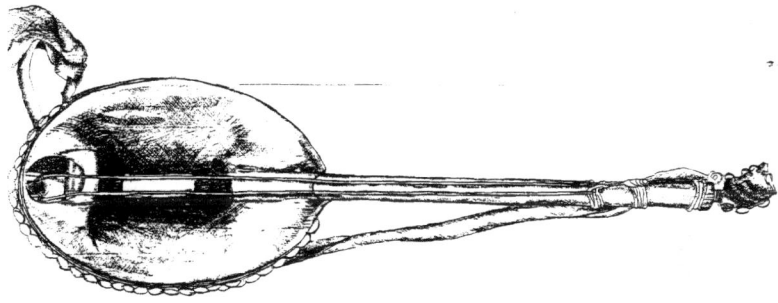

Fig. 25. *Yakandi*

5.6 Conclusion

This chapter has described musical instruments other than the *tsinza* that are present in Bura culture, and has attempted to discuss terminologies used in describing such instruments and the ways they are played. Also, some occasions that require music or in which music may occur but without the

---

79 The Bura believe that twins, triplets or quadruplets are children that belong to a "spirit world". In oder for such children to be free from sicknesses and live a happy life in the world of humans, they must be separated from the "spirit world". *Gulum* music is essential to the rites of the separation.

use of any of the instruments described in this chapter were discussed with examples. It is clear from the discussion in the chapter that not all Bura musical occasions require the use of the instruments described. The chapter also demonstrates that some Bura words or terms that relate to music making are also used in everyday language to describe different things, actions and concepts that reflect some of the beliefs and value system of the society.

It could, therefore, be said that it is not only in the case of the construction of the *tsinza* that special Bura terminologies are used; other Bura instruments also have terminologies used in describing them and their way of playing. In the case of the *tsinza*, we have seen that human attributes are given to the instrument (cf. Chapter 4). The seven slabs are considered to be *mji* people, with each one representing a *kuraku* voice that is required to "communicate" with one another in a "nice" manner. The other Bura instruments are in a similar manner interrelated with activities of the society and in some instances used also as a means of "communication". It is certain that like the *tsinza*, the terminologies used in relation to the other instruments are important in understanding some aspects of the Bura worldview as well. In the next chapter, I turn to the *tsinza* in its traditional context: its use in Bura funerals.

6 The *Tsinza* in its Traditional Context

6.1 Introduction

The *tsinza* occupies a special position in Bura culture. It is used in connection with important ceremonies, especially funerals, and closely linked with Bura identity. Even though the instrument has nowadays assumed other roles with entirely different meanings for many in society, it is believed originally to be an important funerary instrument, as elder musicians of the instrument emphasized to me during my fieldwork.

The traditional repertoire of Bura funerals, however, varies according to region, clan, age, gender and social status. While the rites performed at the funeral of the Bura generally appear to be similar in all the various Bura regions, it is not so when it comes to the music that accompanies the rites. The differences mainly concern the choice of the lead or principal instrument used at funerals. The Bura people who live along the Hawul Valley (East Bura) use *ganga* (drum) as the principal instrument, while among those in the West, the *tsinza* is the principal instrument. In the case of the East Bura, the *ganga* is mostly accompanied by the *tsinza;* while in the case of the West Bura, the *tsinza* is rarely accompanied by the *ganga*. Since the focus of this thesis is the *tsinza*, the data that I will present in this chapter will therefore relate more to the West Bura.

Funerals within Northeast Nigeria are found to be one rite within an inter-related ritual complex pertaining to several domains: death itself, inheritance, ancestralization, and the relationship between the dead and the living. Several rites are performed within each of the domains to safely ensconce the spirit of the dead to the ancestral world. Many of the rites are accompanied by music. The focus of this chapter, therefore, is to look into Bura funerals generally and to discuss the traditional repertoire of Bura funerals, looking into the aspects of its continuity and change. I, however, begin the chapter with a review of some of the anthropological theories that relate to death and some literature that are of interest to this thesis.

Human behavior as it relates to death has been of crucial importance to many of the central theoretical development in anthropology throughout the existence of the discipline. Theories that relate to the rites of passage are of particular interest for this thesis. Van Gennep (1960) deals with funerals as one of a large class of rituals. His thesis is that all rituals involving passage from one state to another share in a single tripartite structure defined by the necessary function of separation from one status and re-incorporation into the new one, with a marginal or liminal period in between. As put by Metcalf and Huntington (1991: 30), "at first sight, the proposition seems innocuous enough, merely the assertion that rites have a beginning, a middle, and an end." But van Gennep was the first to notice just how similar the beginnings, middles, and ends of an extraordinarily wide range of rituals are. He emphasizes that these similarities are not random analogies, but part of single, general phenomena. The general structure underlying a great variety of ritual behavior relates to the social function of recruiting and incorporating individuals who mature, age, and die into a fixed system of culturally defined roles and statuses. According to him, this function is made necessary by the fact that society outlasts the individuals who comprise it.

In their work, Metcalf and Huntington (1991) explore the significance of death in various cultures, including Borneo, Madagascar, ancient Egypt, and Renaissance France, by analyzing the extraordinary variety in their death rituals. By unraveling the rituals of burial and exhumation as well as elaborate rites surrounding royal deaths, the authors demonstrate the way in which each culture's set of burial customs is an expression of its core values regarding the nature of the individual and of life.

In the chapters of part two "Death as transition", Metcalf and Huntington look at the kinds of ethnographic case material that led Hertz (1907) and van Gennep (1960) to stress that death is a gradual process. Death for many peoples represents a process, which begins with the spirit of the person becoming safely ensconced in the ancestral world. It is to this end that many funeral rites are directed. Metcalf and Huntington produce a diagrammatic representation of Hertz' explanation of the symbolic significance of activities surrounding death as a product of three sets of relationships (see fig. 26).

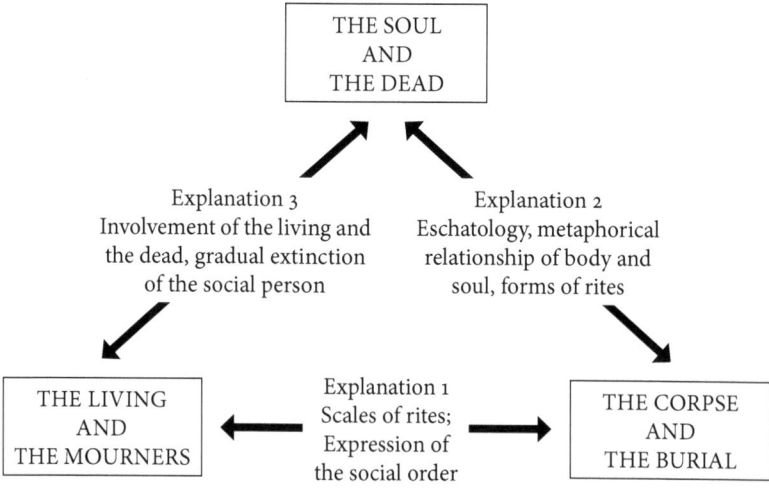

Fig. 26. Schematic diagram of Hertz's arguments (Metcalf and Huntington 1991: 83)

The first explanation (focusing on the relationship between the living vis-à-vis the recently deceased) deals with why the funeral rites of different categories of people vary in many societies. For example, this explanation sheds light on the correlation between the status of the deceased and degrees of elaboration of his or her funeral. The second explanation (focusing on the relationship between the corpse and the soul of the deceased) enhances one's understanding of the meaning of mortuary rituals. This could be achieved by paying attention to the details of the corpse. As David puts it, "this is apprehended through metaphor that is developed into the symbolism of the rites (e.g. sleep with awakening to resurrection, germination or even fermentation)" (David 1992:182).

The third explanation (focusing on the relationship between the living mourners and the soul of the deceased) enables one to understand the rites performed for transformation or extinction of the deceased's social persona.

In any one society, the three pairs of relationships in the Hertzian triangle are all interdependent expressions of the same ideology; no one of the relationships can be understood in isolation. The Hertzian triangle as explained by Metcalf and Huntington is valuable to this chapter in that their commentary on it offers an understanding of some of the rituals performed at Bura funerals even though music is not discussed in their work.

From another perspective, Radcliffe-Brown (1964) based his entire theory of society on the ritual expression of sentiments. According to him, all ritual activity, including funeral rites in whatever form and style, serves to channel sentiments of social bonding and support the organization of society.

The custom of burying the dead in African societies has been a subject of study by many scholars. However, it has been remarkably little studied from an ethnological as opposed to a sociological viewpoint. In Africa generally, death is perceived as the beginning of a person's deeper relationship with all of creation, the complementing of life and the beginning of the communication between the visible and the invisible worlds. The goal of life for many in African societies is to become an ancestor after death. This is the reason why a "correct" funeral must be given to every person that dies; otherwise the person becomes a wandering ghost, unable to "live" properly thereby being a potential danger to the living.

Wilson (1939) was one of the first anthropologists who attempted a systematic analysis of the emotional aspect of funerals in Africa based on firsthand experience. According to him, emotions may be vague and irrational. However, when the analyst knows the culture and particular participants, and has him- or herself shared in the events and, furthermore, is extremely scrupulous of the level of verifiability of each piece of evidence, then the study of the emotional aspect of life yields great dividends.

Bradbury (1965) describes the funeral rites performed for a man who is survived by one or more sons among the Edo people[80] of southwestern Nigeria. His paper could be divided into two main parts: the first dealing with the relationship of parent and child, as well as the relationship of the first son with his siblings, and the second dealing with the mortuary rites, where he describes the various stages involved.

Edo mortuary ritual varies according to the social status and circumstances of the deceased. The older a man is, the more descendants he has, the higher his rank and prestige, the more acceptable his death become. The peaceful demise of an old chief with numerous progeny is as much an occasion for rejoicing is his life's achievement as for sorrow. To die childless, or sonless, is the most dreaded fate. In Edo mortuary rites, the supreme obligation of the eldest son is to bury his father and install or re-dedicate a shrine at which to serve him as an ancestor.

Bradbury's paper indicates that mortuary rites play a crucial role in the on-going processes of lineage and family development. Its emphasis is thus on the type of relationship referred to above in connection with Hertz' explanation no. 3 (the rites performed for transformation or extinction of the deceased's social persona). However, it does not deal with any other relationship other than that of the patrilineal line.

David (1992) examines traditional disposal of the dead in the central Mandara Highlands of Cameroon (a region not too far from the Bura) among the southern Mafa, Sirak Cuvok, Hide, Mabas, Wula, and Gemjek. These are peoples living in adjacent villages who share basic concepts and practices of social organization. He concentrates on material aspects of mortuary practices closely associated with the actual disposal of the dead. The dimensions of variations considered include: physical and managerial direction of the funeral, the location and nature of burial grounds, preparation and clothing of the body, tombs and graves, positioning of the body, and grave goods.

The data David presents demonstrate that the vast majority of the material aspects of disposal of the dead are intimately linked with ideas, values, attitudes, and themes that are also expressed in many different aspects of the lives of the societies he studied. Furthermore, it is clear from his paper that fundamental features of the belief system are shared by all the societies studied. Also apparent is the great variability in the data and the fact that the seven groups choose to emphasize different aspects of this common ideological heritage in differing ways and in different dimensions of mortuary practice. Unlike Bradbury, David's work deals with all the three aspects of the Hertzian triangle. However, he limits himself to the material aspect of burial rites and pays no attention to the role of music in the rites.

---

80   The predominant ethnic group in Nigeria's Delta State.

The role of music in funerals is generally unexplored in many of the studies carried out on the subject in West Africa. Some of the studies that have
paid attention to it (Strumpf 1970, 1976; Aning 1989; Bragner 1993; Mensah
1967a, 1967b, 1993; Saighoe 1984; Vercelli 2006; Wiggins and Kobom 1992;
Seavoy 1982; Godsey 1980; 1984) focus on the *gyil*, an instrument played at
funerals and other rituals by some ethnic groups of northwestern Ghana,
Burkina Faso and Cote d'ivoire (Dagara, Lobi, Birifor and Sisaala). These
studies are important for this thesis in that they offer an insight into the role
of the *gyil* xylophone, which is used in a manner similar to that of the Bura
tsinza at funerals. Both instruments appear to be used as an instrument of
"communication" between the living and the dead.

6.2 Bura Funerals

In order to understand the order of how things happened, and to situate the
traditional repertoire of Bura funerals within the rites performed at funerals
generally, I will first of all give a detailed account of what my informants in
the field described to me as a "Bura funeral". The data presented in this section is, therefore, largely derived from the narratives of my informants, who
include: Kadala Hanku, Yamwada Angili, Kwapchi Audu, and several others
who remain anonymous, as they requested. I also looked into descriptions
contained in the limited scholarly works (Meek, 1931; Davies, 1956) that exists on Bura funerals. The data presented in this chapter on Bura funerals is,
therefore, mainly a collation of the narratives of my informants. I chose to
present the narratives in the "condensed" form in which they appear below,
without specifically quoting directly from anyone of them for the purpose
of clarity. The information they gave was quite similar; therefore, it is more
practical to present it in this manner for this chapter.

I must make it clear that I am aware of the fact that there is no such thing
as a "standard" funeral in any given society. Funerals vary and can be undertaken in different ways. However, as part of my strategy, I reconstructed
what the Bura, as narrated to me by my informants, perceive as their "standard" funerary rites, with the aim of comparing it with a traditional funeral I
observed in the course of fieldwork for this study. The funeral I observed is
presented in this chapter as a case study.

I must equally point out as well that none of the literature (Meek, 1931;
Davies, 1956) that exists on Bura funerals paid any particular attention to its
repertoire. Although there is mention of music being performed here and
there in the course of a funeral, there is no detail provided about what kind
of music is played. The case study that is presented in this chapter is, therefore, very useful in understanding the *tsinza* in its traditional context in that
it makes clear the stages at which *tsinza* music is performed during the rites.

Based on what my informants narrated to me in the field, a detailed description of the funeral of an adult Bura man, the archetypal funeral, is given first, followed by the variations in the funerals of other categories of the Bura mentioned earlier. This is then followed by a case study of indigenous funeral rites I observed.

6.2.1 Funeral Rites of an Adult Bura Man

Among the Bura people, when an old[81] man dies there are many ceremonies which must be performed. The death is not made known to people outside the compound of the dead person until the corpse is prepared: only a few of his close relatives and neighbours are informed. Lamentation or crying does not start immediately. His head is shaved, his body bathed, trousers put on, and a girdle put around his waist as quickly as possible after death. The corpse is laid out on a bed made of reeds (*katsar*), with the head resting on a roll of cloth (*kuntu*).

A goat is killed, guinea corn mush (*Divar mhyi*) is cooked and the compound swept. The husbands of the deceased's daughters are sent to the surrounding villages to make the death known. A *tsinza* (xylophone) is brought to the side of the corpse and struck. A horn player blows his instrument three times and a woman gives three loud screams.[82] It is then that everybody around begins to cry "Wu". *Tsinza* music is played again, a chicken is caught in the deceased's compound, and held by one of the mourners as they go from house to house in the village singing a dirge and dancing.

Some men are sent out to look for a site for the grave in the clan cemetery. Each clan has its own graveyard situated at the outskirts of the village. Sometimes, however, older people request that they be buried in their compound when they die. If such a request is made, it is usually respected.

When a gravesite is chosen, hoes, axes, and gourds are collected and a special axe handle is carved for the digging of the grave. A goat is killed for the gravediggers. It must be roasted and eaten on the spot. A large pot is brought and filled with *Mbal* (sorghum beer) for the gravediggers. The gravediggers are usually comprised of the husbands of the deceased's daughters, some of his relatives, and a traditional undertaker who is usually invited. The digging goes on with the playing of music and drinking of *Mbal*. Throughout the duration of the digging of the grave, special tunes *tsá la kula* -music for grave digging and, *Sikba* - music to assuage the grief of the mourners are played by the *tsinza* musicians.

---

81 Age 50 years and above.
82 The numbers "3" and "4" are used for gender differentiation in Bura society –particularly in rituals. "3" is associated with male, while "4" is associated with female.

In most cases, a dying man requests that one of his sons or a close friend of his strike the spot for the grave. The topsoil is removed first, and then a small hole is made, through which a body may pass, and reaching through the mouth of the grave hollows out the grave. When the digging of the grave is finished, the gravediggers return to the deceased's compound with the beating of *tsinza*, loud singing, and a marching dance (*dzakwa-dzakwa*). Upon reaching the compound, they go straight to the room of the deceased and perform *bathla tuwa* (funeral dance) at the front of the room.

The digging of the grave usually takes a whole day, depending on the nature of the soil. Sometimes the gravediggers encounter rocks,[83] which will force them to abandon the digging and start all over again at a new spot. While the digging goes on, other ceremonies take place in the deceased's compound.

If the dead person had wealth, his eldest son spreads his best clothes and gowns over the veranda roof under which the deceased usually dressed. The clothes and gowns are removed immediately once the corpse is buried. The husbands of his daughters, tie strips of cotton cloth (*kuntu*) about the fence or compound. They also provide *kuntu*, which is cut into pieces by the daughters of the deceased and decorated with cowry shells and coins. This is called *kisingil* (headband), and the daughters of the deceased tie them around their heads throughout the mourning period. Also, the young women of the community who are close friends of daughters of the deceased provide them with *jigida* (waist beads) to be worn around their necks.

The deceased's quiver of arrows and his bows are brought and men take their turns with his bows in a mock war dance (*fil ncabwi*). A dancer races to and fro and leaps into the air with a shriek as he draws back the bow in preparation to shoot.

The deceased is dressed in his best clothes. Two of his best *bull* (gowns), a cap, and a turban are put on him. The corpse is then taken out and presented to the crowd for them to see what fine clothes he has in which to be buried. The presentation of the corpse is also done to prove to the community that the deceased did not engage in witchcraft. Deaths, sicknesses, and misfortunes are in the people' belief system, caused by witches. When a man who is a warlock dies, he bloats all over the body. When people see this, it is a sign that the deceased was a witch. To prove their innocence, older men often request that their corpses be left from sundown to sundown after their death. If blood runs out of the deceased's mouth and nose, it is evidence of bloating—and there can be no question that he was possessed.

After the presentation of the corpse, it is taken and seated against the deceased's granary. (Men and women have separate granaries.) Farm implements are also placed before it. The roof of the granary is removed and

---

83   Most area of Bura land is hilly in nature (see Chapter 3).

the deceased's eldest daughter climbs in and pulls out the heads of guinea corn. As she then climbs down from the granary, *Kukula* (farming) music is performed by the musicians at this stage. The deceased's daughter tosses the seeds of the guinea corn into the air. About four young men, holding hoes, dance to the tune being played by the musicians, demonstrating how farming is done. People around also rush for the seeds that are tossed into the air.

The symbolism of this dance performed for an old man represents his life's last planting. It also perhaps represents regeneration and growth. In the same way as crops are planted, so also is the body of a deceased person buried. The *mambula* is reincorporated into the ancestral world later. The seeds tossed into the air during the *kukula* dance are believed to promote fertility when mixed with seeds to be planted during the next farming season. This belief is derived from the fact that the seeds are pulled out of the deceased's full granary against which the corpse is rested for the dance. It is, however, important to note that if the granary is full to the brim when its roof is removed, the deceased is praised for hard work. To avoid being mocked by members of the community, the deceased's children and close relatives always make sure that their father's granary is kept full whenever they notice that his death is inevitable.

After the *kukula* dance, the most senior wife of the deceased uproots her *gilam*, a large water storage pot, and turns it upside down. She also collects the *kugwa diva* (calabash) she used to serve her deceased husband's meal inside the house, and brings it before the seated corpse and smashes it. She returns to her hut without turning back to look at the corpse. Our understanding of the symbolic meaning of the rites that immediately follow the *kukula* dance is enhanced by Hertz' third explanation—the relationship between the living mourners and the soul of the deceased (especially the social persona aspect of his soul) which is undergoing transformation (see fig. 26)—and by van Gennep's paradigm for rites of separation. The uprooting of the deceased's most senior wife's water pot and the smashing of his eating calabash (*kugwa diva*) marks the beginning of gradual disentanglement of the deceased with his social persona.

After the kukula dance and the smashing of the deceased's eating calabash by his most senior wife, the corpse is then placed on a cornstalk platform carried by about four to six men. The procession marches the corpse through the compound three times. One of the deceased's grandsons holds a rooster and walks ahead of the procession. As they go around the house, the corpse is taken into the women's compound, starting with the most senior wife—each wife has her own hut, in front of which is a stack of wood. This enables the wives to see their husband for the last time. It is also done so that the deceased can "see" his compound for the last time. After the third go around, the rooster's head is dashed against the compound entrance post and thrown away. Children rush for it, roast it, and share the meat amongst them; though, the deceased's children and grandchildren are prohibited from eating the meat.

The cornstalk fence on the left hand side of the compound entrance is pulled down and outwards. The corpse is taken out of the compound through the broken fence. Immediately as the corpse is taken out of the compound, joking relations[84] (*mjir sardzi*) of the deceased may seize the corpse. It is taken to where the deceased usually spent his leisure time while alive; along the way to his farm, and on the path to the market he used to frequent. It is important to note that the older a person is, and the more "normal" the corpse is, the more *mjir sardzi* play with it, by taking it to the deceased's haunts while alive.

After this, the corpse is carried to the grave with the playing of *tsinza* music, loud singing, and a marching dance (*dzakwa-dzakwa*). Men carry their bows, quivers, spears, and axes. These are raised into the air as they sing and dance, some in front of those carrying the corpse and others at the back. At the grave, one of the *mjir sardzi* blocks the grave by entering and lying in it. A Bura shirt (*Dan ciki*) and a cap (*dzakwa*) must be given to him as compensation before he comes out of the grave.

A man who knows how to take a corpse into a grave enters first and receives the corpse and lays it properly. The laying of the corpse is accompanied by *tsinza* music. The *tsinza* musician, directs the person laying the corpse through his music on how to go about it. The corpse is laid on a special Bura mat (*zibil*) provided by the husband of a daughter—usually the most senior daughter—of the deceased. A man's corpse is laid prostrate on his right side with the head to the south, facing east, and the right hand placed under the head.[85] *Kugwa Ciba,* a calabash, is placed on a shelf above the deceased man's head for his use in the afterlife. He then comes out of the grave, and the mouth of the grave is closed by a large, flat stone, which has also been provided by the husband of the most senior daughter of the deceased. Fresh mud is plastered about the stone to seal the mouth of the grave. Amidst *tsinza* music, earth is shoveled on top of the grave until a mound is formed. When the grave has been heaped up, the gourd used in shoveling earth out of the grave is placed on top of the mound and smashed. Someone picks up the axe handle used in digging the grave and strikes the ground with it three times. One such blow is struck above the head, one on the right side, and the other on the left side of the grave. The wooden handle

---

84 The great grand children of first cousins become joking relations in Bura culture. The relationship is such that one is by custom permitted to tease or make fun of the other without anyone taking offence.

85 This position of the corpse, in Bura worldview, has to do with the way a husband and wife sleep. It is with the left hand that the husband, lying on his right side, claps his wife in bed. Wives, and by implication women, sleep on their left side.

of the axe is detached from the metal head and then placed on the mound. A dear friend of the dead takes an arrow from his quiver and rushes about the grave and shoots it. Small children make a dash for it, and the first one to reach the spot gets the arrow.

The procession, still amidst the playing of *tsinza* music, then returns to the compound of the deceased. Upon reaching the compound, the mourners go right into the compound and dance the "death dance" (*bathla mshi*). After this, the mourners move out of the compound and dance the mourners' dance (*bathla tuwa*). The relatives of the deceased then tell the sons-in-law to dance in honor of the deceased father of their wives. They must also dance on specific occasions through the first night after the burial. If they refuse to dance on any occasion, they are asked to drink bitter water. If they refuse the bitter water, they must pay two rolls of *kuntu* (cloth) as a fine for their insubordination.

A forked branch of *Nfur ntursha* (wild berry tree) is cut and planted into the ground in front of the deceased's room. The man who has been appointed temporary head of the household for the duration of the funeral rites by the deceased's relatives is responsible for having food set out each day and each night for the deceased's *mambula* (soul). The food is kept in a calabash in the forked tree branch.

When the first night is over, a chicken is killed and the roof of the house in which the deceased died is lifted off. Then everyone goes to his or her own home. On the third day people gather again for the *kil mbwa Humbutu* (taking *Humbutu* into the deceased's compound) ceremony; a ceremony in which a *Humbutu* (funerary pot) is brought into the deceased's compound by his relatives. The deceased's most senior son-in-law provides a chicken, which is slaughtered and cooked. This is served with mush in the *Humbutu*, which is placed in front of the deceased's room. Again, this rite is accompanied by *tsinza* music.

After a while, the appointed head of the house makes beer for the *Hir kula* ceremony—the rites of plastering over the top of the grave and surrounding it with a stone circle. At this ceremony, he calls together the sons-in-law and divides the work of *Kuri tuwa* (finishing the mourning) amongst them. Two goats are to be brought, and a few chickens, several gowns, flour, salt, cloth, butter, and *msha* (red earth) also must be provided. The helpers, who are friends of the sons-in-law, must provide a small *nciwa* (male goat) and two chickens. When each has learned his duty, he goes his way until the head of the household tells them it's time.

When the appointed head of the house is about ready for the *Kuri tuwa*, usually two to three months after the death, he sends word to all who are to provide help for the last mourning, and says that he is ready to thresh the beer corn and that everything should be ready by the following Friday. The beer corn is threshed on one Friday and the *Kuri tuwa* is held on the next Friday.

Before the *Kuri tuwa* ceremony, the appointed head of the house goes to each wife and asks her whom she would like to inherit her as a wife.[86] The women must make their choice among the relatives of the deceased husband. They are not permitted to choose outside of his family. The women give him the names of the men and he will then go and inform those men. These men whose names have been mentioned will also make beer and bring a goat each for the wives they are to receive. I must make it clear here that the wives do have the right not to re-marry. In most cases, older women choose not to re-marry after the death of their husband. If a wife chooses not to re-marry, she remains in her hut in the compound for the rest of her life.

On the *vir livi tuwa* (the day before the *Kuri tuwa*) all the relatives of the deceased come, some with goats and some with chickens. They bring them and kill them at the entrance to the dead relative's compound. The husbands of the daughters bring large goats. If their goats are not very large, they are refused. Sometimes a small goat is accepted if a roll of *kuntu* is tied around its neck. A prayer is said to repose the *mambula* (soul) of the deceased and the animals are slaughtered. When their goats are killed, a shoulder, one side of the ribs, and the back rump are given to the new head of household. A leg and the front of the rump are given to the mother of each wife. The backbone is given to the deceased's brothers. As part of this day's rituals, the young women and their friends rub their bodies with *mal fuma* (sheabutter) and *msha* (red ochre soil)

All who kill any animal at the mourning must bring a leg of goat or a leg of chicken to the forked branch of *ntursha* planted in front of the deceased's room. This is where the deceased's *mambula* (soul) "eats". The beer is strained and all present drink until some begin to stagger as they dance to *tsinza* music. Later that night, all of the relatives who have come to the mourning go home. The property of the deceased is not divided until everyone has slept and come back the next morning. The eldest son, however, receives most of the property.

If the one who dies has no children old enough to take his place and not even old enough to be engaged, an important person in the family will take charge of his property until the children are grown. When they are grown, he will turn all the property of the deceased back to them. Such property would include the house, farm, animals, *etc.* The person who assumes this responsibility also takes the quiver of the deceased and assumes responsibility for his debts. The debtors all appear on the final day of *Kuri two* and ask for their debts to be paid. If the debt is valid and many know that it is a true debt, it is paid at once. Those debtors who do not have many witnesses

---

86   The Bura practiced wife inheritance before the inception of Christianity in the area.

as to the validity of their debt have to drink "medicine"[87] to assure the family that the debt is valid. If they refuse to drink "medicine" the debt can never be brought up again. The debtors loose because they have no witnesses and they are afraid to risk being their own witnesses by drinking poison.

On the *Kuri tuwa* day, all the sticks, cornstalks, *kisingil* (head bands), and the stand used during the burial day are collected and dumped at a *matingdla* (fork in the road). When all is finished, the wives go to their new homes and the children go to the homes in which they are to be reared—children are given stepfathers among the deceased's lineage members. But before the wives and children disperse to their new homes, a *haptu* (personal god pot or other empowered item) or a *mufil* (blacksmith's hammer) is placed on their heads three times each to protect them against witches. The children are often spoken of as *musta* (the fatherless) and the wives as *mwala kifa* (inherited wives).

6.2.2 Funeral Rites of an Adult Bura Woman

The ceremonies performed at the funeral rites of an adult Bura woman follows a similar pattern to that of an adult Bura man in many aspects. However, aspects that emphasizes gender differences are strictly adhered to in the course of a funeral.

For a woman, in preparing the body, the head is not shaved. Instead the hair is plaited and her clothes put on—a striped cloth known as *japta*. As in the case of a man, if she was wealthy, the deceased's most senior daughter spreads her best clothes over the roof of the veranda under which the corpse is kept. In the case of a woman, *japta* are spread instead of *bull* (gowns).

If the deceased is a widow who never married after the death of her first husband, a *fil ncabwi* (mock war dance) is performed during her funeral as a mark of honor. When a man dies his wives are asked to choose whom they want to take them. This dance is performed as a mark of honour to a deceased man because during his lifetime he was the sole provider and protector of his family. The dance shows how "manly" (*sal kur*) the deceased had been. In this light, the dance is also performed for a widow who never re-married after the death of her first husband to honor, it is said, the fact that she lived in accordance to the expectation set up for men by assuming the responsibility that prior was carried out by her husband. In Bura society, it is the absolute responsibility of men to provide food, shelter and clothing for all members of their household. Women engage in farming, but it is at their own discretion to contribute to their farm produce to feed the

---

87 Form of oath taking that delibrately involves drinking a posinous substance to prove innocence or justify rightfulness.

family. Otherwise, they choose what to do with their farm produce. Therefore, by assuming the responsibility that is considered to be that of a man, a woman who never remarried after the death of her husband is honored with such a dance.

A woman who remarries after the death of her first husband does not receive such a dance. This is because by remarrying, her new husband assumes the responsibility of catering for all her needs. She leaves her old home and moves to a new household under the control of a man. She is, therefore, not qualified to receive *fil ncabwi* dance at her funeral.

Although women engage in farming, it is seen as a man's job. Therefore, when a woman dies, *kukula* (farming dance) is not performed. Other ways in which a woman's funeral differs from that of a man's is that her corpse is neither marched through the compound nor taken out through a broken fence, as a woman cannot be the head of a compound.

For an old woman, the corpse is carried to the grave amidst women carrying decorated calabashes and gourds—smaller, decorated calabashes which are carefully arranged inside larger ones. The carrying of the corpse to the grave is accompanied by the playing of *tsinza*, loud singing, and a marching dance. The *tsinza* tune played while carrying the corpse of an old woman to the grave is the same as that played for an old man. The tune (*para*) requires a marching dance that is considered fit for such a procession. However, men do not carry their bows and quivers. Such weapons are associated with men and should not be displayed when a woman's corpse is being taken to the grave.

Once at the grave, the deceased's corpse is laid prostrate on her left side with the head to the south, facing west, and the left hand under the head. An oil container (*kutuku*) is placed in a calabash and placed on a shelf above her head. This is different from a man's funeral, where *kutuku* is not used.

For a woman, after the grave has been mounded up and the gourd used in shovelling earth out of the grave has been smashed on top of it, someone picks up the axe handle used in the digging and strikes the ground with it four times, instead of three as in a man's case. One blow is struck above the head, one each on the left and right side, and one below the feet. The wooden handle of the axe is detached and then placed on the mound. In the case of a woman, an arrow is not shot over the grave.

If a deceased woman has children, her children's heads are not rounded with *haptu* or *mufil* (personal god or blacksmith's hammer) on the final day of *Kuri tuwa*, as is the case when a man dies. The property of a deceased woman is shared among her children and sisters. If she has no children, her sisters inherit all her property; a man does not inherit his wife's property.

6.2.3 Funeral Rites of a Young Bura

Unlike in the case of an old man, the death of a young person is a very sad event.[88] Lamentation or crying by the immediate family members of the deceased starts at once when such a death occurs. As the dead body lies in the hut, the mother and her close female relatives chant a funeral dirge. Other relatives (male) sit in a circle in front of the compound.

The digging of the grave of a young person is done without music. The corpse is washed and prepared as the grave is being dug. If the deceased is married, his or her best clothes (*bull* for a man, *japta* for a woman) are put on. If the deceased is an infant, the corpse is wrapped in *kuntu*. In contrast to the funerals of the elderly, the corpse is brought out for burial as soon as the grave is ready.

If the deceased is male and married and lives in his own compound, the fence of the compound is smashed. The corpse is taken out through the smashed portion of the fence. If male and married but still living in his father's compound, the corpse is taken out through the compound entrance. Female corpses, whether married or not, are not taken out through a broken fence.

To the accompaniment of weeping and wailing, the corpse is taken to the grave for burial. The iron axe-head used in the digging is removed from the wooden handle and put in a flame to purge the pollution of death. The handle is left lying across the grave.

No other ceremony is performed until on the seventh day. If the deceased (male or female) is married, a goat is slaughtered; if unmarried and below the age of 35, some porridge is made on the seventh day.

If the deceased is male, his children are either given to his brothers or to his father. If they are considered to be too young, they are left with their mother. The wife is asked whom of the deceased's brothers she would like to stay with. Her decision is, however, subject to approval by the senior lineage members. The person that inherits her takes her with her children if they are considered too young to be separated from her. The older children are given to the deceased's father.

If the deceased is a woman, her children and sisters inherit her property. The children are handed over to co-wives if the man is polygamous, or are taken over by her sisters, depending on the decision of the man and his senior lineage members. The children come back to their father's lineage when they are considered old enough.

---

88   There is the realization that dying young means not enjoying the full fruits of life.

6.2.4 Funeral Rites of a Chief

When a chief (*kuhyi*) dies, the death is not immediately made known until such a time that the members of the royal family are satisfied with the preparations made for the burial. At this time, the death is only made known to a few people: these people must be members of the royal family. Similar preparations to those of an old person are made. But in the case of a *kuhyi* (or any other royal person, whether male or female) only members of the royal family can touch, or even go near, the corpse. While shaving the head, the *jigwar* (pigtail) is cut off. This will be plaited into the hair of the successor to the deceased *kuhyi*.

In the case of a *kuhyi*, it is only a royal daughter (*kwatam*), or a woman married to a royal person, who gives three loud screams after the death is made known. This is different from that of an old man, when all work in the community must stop.

Meanwhile, a grave is being dug and the blacksmiths are working on the *kulahu lia* (iron stool) and *mirlalang* (Y-shaped props, also made of iron), which will be used in the burial. The forging of the *mirlalang* and the *kulahu lia* is accompanied by *tsinza* music, and is done outside the chief's compound, inside which the grave will also be dug.

When coming for the funeral, men dress in their best *bull* (gown), carrying spears, bows and quivers. They tie their *bull* at the waist with a strip of *kuntu*. Upon reaching the compound of the deceased, they hang their bows and quivers on a tree in front of the compound. They go into the compound to salute the members of the deceased's family and then come back out to sit in front of the compound.

Unlike in the case of an old, non-royal person, a royal corpse is not to be presented to the members of the community when it is ready for burial. Among the Bura people, chiefs are buried in a seated position. The corpse is placed on the *kulahu lia* (iron stool). A *Mirlalang* (Y-shaped props) is placed under the arms, knees, and back of the neck. Charcoal is sprinkled freely in the grave and over the body, purportedly as a protection against termites, by which the corpse of a *kuhyi* is not supposed to be touched. The head is, however, not covered with charcoal. A red cap and a turban are placed onto the head. A specially made *tuhum lia* (metal pot) is placed over the turbaned head, resting on the shoulders.

The *hir kula* and *kuri tuwa* ceremonies of a chief take place just as in the case of an old, non-royal person. However, the whole community participates in the ceremonies. The successor of the deceased *kuhyi* and heads of the various clans in the village make sacrifices on behalf of the members of their clans. For the *hir kula* and *kuri tuwa* ceremonies, members of each clan and sons-in-law of the deceased *kuhyi* each bring a goat, several chickens and several rolls of *kuntu*. Children of the deceased and other members of the royal family present a cow. The goats, chicken, and cow are slaughtered. The heart and kidney of the cow are presented by the children of the deceased and then are cooked and left overnight in the deceased's room as an offering. It is believed that the deceased's soul (*mambula*) appears and eats the soul (*mambula*) of the food. On the next day, the food is removed and eaten by the children of the deceased *kuhyi*.

6.2.5 Funeral Rites of Blacksmiths

Blacksmiths are honoured among the Bura people.[89] Smiting is a special preserve of the *Mshelia/Kengal* clan. Blacksmiths are buried in the same way in which a chief is buried.[90] When a blacksmith dies, word is sent to all neighbouring blacksmiths. They come with their working tools to perform the art of their departed colleague, and a forge is set in front of the deceased's compound. The blacksmiths swear an oath not to harm each other in the process of displaying their skills. It is a moment of public display of 'skillfulness' in the art of smiting as some of them use bare hands to take red-hot iron from the forge and even stretch it. It is during such a public display of 'skillfulness' that the *kulahu lia* (iron stool) and *mirlalang* (Y-shaped props) required for the burial are made. The rite of making the *mirlalang* and *kulahu lia* is accompanied by *tsinza* music (*tsa kithla – kithla*) played specifically at the funeral of blacksmiths.

A blacksmith is buried in a sitting position, with a *kulahu lia* put under the buttocks and *mirlalang* placed under the arms, knees, and back of the neck. Charcoal is freely sprinkled in the grave and over the body.

6.3 Repertoire of Bura Funerals—A Case Study

From the description of the funerals presented above, it is certain that *tsinza* music plays an important role in the rites performed at indigenous Bura funerals. It accompanies almost all the stages of the rites performed. The entire repertoire performed at funerals consists of instrumental pieces. The pieces are, however, described by specific titles and played in specific sequence during funerals. None of the scanty literatures on Bura funerals

---

89 To the Bura they are honored because as iron smelters and smiths, they manufacture hoes, the most important of all Bura tools.

90 They are buried like chiefs in a sitting position, because just as chiefs watch over their people and land, the blacksmiths watch over the food production of the society.

discussed the repertoire performed at such occasions. Mostly, it is merely mentioned that music is performed at certain stages of some rites.

While on one of the several fieldwork visits I undertook for this thesis in 2009, a master musician of the *tsinza*, Kida Kanti, died and was given an indigenous Bura funeral. Aged about 70 years old, Kanti neither converted to Christianity nor Islam, the two major religions that have been adopted by many in the area. He practiced Bura traditional religion and was according-ly buried in the traditional way. This gave me the chance of observing some of the rites performed at his funeral held in his compound at Billa village.[91]

At the time I arrived at his funeral, the grave was being dug right in-side his compound in the shaft and tunnel form of the Bura grave. There were five *tsinza* musicians performing funeral tunes as the grave was be-ing dug. Some men were seated outside the compound while some stood where the grave was being dug. Whilst the *tsinza* music is instrumental, I needed someone who could interpret to me the meanings of the rhyth-mic text spoken on it since the Bura recognizes it as "speech". I spotted one of the musicians with whom I had earlier conducted several interviews on the instrument, Buba Nganjiwa, and sat next to him as he was not one of those performing at that occasion. This gave me the opportunity to ask him questions as the funeral went on. As I sat with him, I asked about the *tsinza* music being played at that moment I arrived. He explained to me that the music being played at that stage of the funeral was *Sikba*. According to him:

> "These are songs that are played to support the family and relatives in their pain. It equally serves as a means of communication to inform people of a death in the community. Wherever people are, when *sikiba* music is heard being played, it means that an old person has died in the community. Work in the community must stop immediately with people proceeding to the de-ceased's compound to sympathize with the family and participate in the cer-emonies. If it were in the olden days, this piece of music would have been played with children following the musicians and singing around the com-munity... Our people don't like these things again" (Nganjiwa, personal com-munication, 2004).

Asked what song the children would have sung while following the *tsinza* musicians from compound to compound to make the death known, Ngan-jiwa sang along the tune being played by the musicians:

1. *Kaka ya...*
   Oh... grandfather...

---

91 One of the several southern Bura-speaking people's villages where I conducted fieldwork for this study.

2. *Aya kaka ya kaka ngilan*
   Oh... great grandfather
3. *Kaka wa ana jakta ali*
   Who will give me such a grandfather again.
4. *Aya kaka ya kaka ngilan*
   Oh... great grandfather.

He explained that the *sikiba* tune is a "conversation" between the deceased person and the living, with the *tsinza* player serving as the facilitator of the "conversation." For the Bura, according to him, *tsinza* music is a music that is understood in the ancestral world. As the deceased departs to the ancestral world, he "communicates" with the mourners through the *tsinza* music. This seems to refer to the rhythmic phrases played on the instrument understood by the people as speech.

After playing this particular tune for a while, the music changed. Nganjiwa was quick to point out to me that the tune the musicians changed to was the deceased's "response". He sang along:

1. Madar ma na an lihir na
   My mother's children this is my departure for home
2. Bzir ma na an lihir na
   My brother this is my departure for home
3. Mwalankiya ya an lihir na
   My wife this is my departure for home
4. Aya... mburu a kiba kira wa
   Oh no... we shall not meet again
5. Mdir ki an lihar na..
   My boss this is my departure for home...

He explained that this song could go on and on, mentioning the names of the deceased's children, friends and relatives, all with the intention of expressing that he bids them farewell.[92] The response of the family after this song depends on the circumstances surrounding the death. For example, if the deceased died leaving behind young children, the response would center on showing concern for who takes care of them now that their father is dead.

In the case of Kanti, he died towards the end of the rainy season. In response to him informing his wives, brothers, children and relations of his departure, the tune that followed the earlier one went:

---

92 Meaning that it can be performed for a long period mentioning all the acquintances of deceased to "inform" them of his "departure".

1. Ga mti ni
   Now that you died
2. Saka liha wa
   It is not time to go home
3. Wa an ta si wula fakuyeri ni ri?
   Who is going to take care of the farms?
4. Aya... su ku wuta ra...
   Oh no... Something bad has befallen me...

After the above tunes were repeated over and over, the music gradually turned into the praises of the deceased all considered to be part of the sikba songs. Kanti's good qualities were extolled in various tunes:

1. Dau.. Kumandi nungtung
   Long... God the big one
2. Waiya... (2×)
   Oh... (2×)
3. Wu.. kumandi nugntung
   Wide... God the very big one
4. Waiya... (2×)
   Oh... (2×)
5. Kumi gandi kula fang nda
   White beard without any spot
6. Waiya... (2×)
   Oh... (2×)

Kanti was praised in this manner because according to Nganjiwa, among the Bura, as an aged man becomes older, he becomes more of a god. And when his years are heavy upon him he is almost a deity. Kanti, by his age was considered a very old person; therefore, he was given the attributes of a god. God is considered to be long, big and wide. As a man gets older, he is considered to possess wide and deep knowledge. So as far as Kanti's case was concerned, by being an old person, he possessed such a quality.

In the next song, Kanti was praised for being someone who could open the path of well-being for the members of his family here on earth. As he had passed on, he was considered to have gone ahead of the living and his soul mambula was better situated to continue to open the doors of well being for them. The song went:

1. Diya abur ma vir ku kuri
   If the days are over
2. Ayee... ee yalla (3×)
   Oh... Yeah

3. Mjir Jangulang ata kila ri ala mburu laku
   The people of Jangulang (land of ancestors) would make a way for us
4. Mburu ata wuta barka
   We would receive blessings
5. Ayee...ee yalla
   Oh... Yeah

Soon after it was made known that the digging of the grave was completed and Kanti's corpse prepared for burial, the *tsinza* music changed to tunes called *Dzakwa—Dzakwa*. The corpse was brought out of the deceased's room and laid under a corn stalk sun shade (*Siva*) in front of it. As the music went on, many of the mourners stood up to dance to the tune. It was a kind of a marching dance with men, women and children going back and forth with clutched fists raised up. Some of the men raised spears while some raised bows. Nganjiwa explained to me that the *Dzakwa—Dzakwa* tune being played was about a "force" that swiftly took Kanti away.[93] The tune asks what that force is. *Duku* (eagle), a bird that lives in a *du* (valley), is considered to be the only "force" that is capable of such an act. For the Bura, *duku* is a bird of great strength and speed. Therefore, if it weren't for a *duku*, it would be difficult to understand how a loved one could be taken away so easily. It implies that among all other things, it is only the *duku* that is capable of such an act. Nothing else could have snatched a loved one but this bird of great strength and speed that can take its prey unawares. The song is a praise demonstrating how important or how attached a deceased is to the mourners, who would have not allowed anything to take away a loved one amongst them. The song went:

1. *Dika...*
   Bird...
2. *Dika du ya?*
   Is it a bird of the valley?
3. *A a a... dika du ya?*
   A a a... Is it a bird of the valley?
4. *Dika ri si ama ri?*
   Where did the bird come from?
5. *Kara kil bzir ali?*
   To take away a son from me?
6. *A a a... dika du ya?*
   A a a... Is it a bird of the valley?

---

93 Death is not considered as a natural happening but always likened to a "force" that is not seen. Such a "force" acts so swiftly to snatch a member of the society from loved ones.

After the Dzakwa—Dzakwa dance, a bathla tuwa (mourning dance) was performed. This was again a tune and dance in honour of Kanti. His "handsomeness" was compared to Hwalang (a specie of snake) that mostly lives on riverbanks. This specie of snake is considered harmless and very "beautiful" because the scales on its body form a beautiful design pattern. Among the Bura, it is forbidden to kill this particular specie of snake.[94] They believe that it protects the compound. In fact, it is a thing of joy when they are spotted within the compound and away from the riverbanks. The death of Kanti was compared to the killing of Hwalang. Just as it is considered cruel to kill this 'beautiful' and 'harmless' creature, so is the departure of Kanti considered cruel. Therefore, in the tune, the mourners were urged to mourn him very well, because he was an "Hwalang" that has departed. The tune went thus:

1. Hwalang mya zirku na
   My riverbank Hwalang
2. A fil fila ata mwari na
   Jumping and going away
3. Aya...yayi
   Oh...yeah
4. Sal ka ki ni (2×)
   A man with a household (2×)
5. Ata mwari ashina
   Is departing today
6. Mburu a tuwa ni bu
   Let us mourn him please
7. Aya...yayi
   Oh...yeah
8. Mburu a tuwa ni
   Let us mourn him
9. Aya...yayi
   Oh...yeah.

The bathla tuwa was followed by fil ncabwi (mock war dance). In this dance, the men took turns brandishing the bow and quiver of the late Kanti. As they limp and race forward, they end up at where the corpse was laid, raising the bow and quiver up into the sky as a salute to the deceased. The tune played for the fil ncabwi went:

1. Sal...
   Man...

---

94 Snakes are considered poisonous and dangerous. Snakes are, therefore, killed the moment any is sighted.

2. *Sal ni sal kazan*
   The man is truly a brave man
3. *Ata mwari ashina*
   He is going today
4. *Sal ni sal*
   The man is truly a brave man

In the tune that accompanied the *fil ncabwi*, Kanti was praised as being a 'man'. The dance was performed as a mark of respect for him, remembering the 'manly' roles he fulfilled while he was alive. One of such 'manly' roles, as explained to me by Nganjiwa, was the ability of Kanti to grow enough crops to cater for his family while alive.

Soon after several men took part in the *fil ncabwi,* the corpse of Kanti was lifted and seated on a mat with the back rested against a granary. The thatched cover of the granary was removed and the *fil ncabwi* dance changed to *Kukula*, a dance representing the clearing of new farmland. Men and women held hoes as they danced in front of the corpse. I noted that the music did not change from the one earlier played for the *fil ncabwi*. Nganjiwa explained to me that the music was the same and that it serves both purposes. According to him the tune is called *Kukula*.[95] "It is a tune that goes with rigorous work. So both dances are performed to indicate how hard working the deceased was while alive. Can't you see that his granary is full of sorghum?" (Nganjiwa, personal communication, 2009).

The *tsinza* music stopped briefly. Several men lifted the corpse and walked around within the compound with it. As soon as it was lifted, the musicians played a tune and the deceased's daughters and female relatives sang along:

1. Msira lai
   I am glad
2. A...yayi...
   Oh...yeah...
3. Msira lai
   I am glad
4. Baba na
   My father
5. Ga msira lai
   You are so sweet to me

---

95 For the symbolic meaning of this dance see the description of the funeral of an adult Bura man above.

The corpse was taken round three times. After the third round, it was taken to the graveside. As those carrying it moved towards where the grave was dug, the *tsinza* tune changed to *Para*. The music went:

1. *Asira mwa a mwari ahar yeru*
   Come let us go to our village
2. *Wa ana mwari akwa di mambula ka jakta nka ri?*
   Who can go to the village of souls and come back?
3. *Diva ni msira*
   Food is so sweet
4. *Iya a mwari wa shang shang wa*
   I will not go at all
5. *Iya a mwari wa shang baba wa*
   I will not go at all my father
6. *Iya a mwari shang wa*
   I will not go at all.

In this song, the deceased person beckoned to the mourners to come and follow him to the land of *Mambula*.[96] But the reply was that nobody wanted to go with him, as no one has ever gone to the land of *Mambula* and returned. Moreover, food is still so sweet; therefore, no one wanted to go to the land of *Mambula*.

Someone climbed into the grave after a chanting of an incantation and pouring sorghum beer over it. The corpse was lowered to the person inside for positioning. As he positioned the corpse inside the grave, Nganjiwa interpreted to me the music played by the *tsinza* player:

1. *Ka mda namta vi vi kir*
   Let the head be positioned well
2. *Ka mda namta vi vi sil*
   Let the legs be positioned well
3. *Sal ni sal kazang*
   What a great man
4. *Salir mwanki yeri*
   Husband to many wives
5. *Baba madankyar yeri*
   Father of many children

The person inside the grave climbed out after positioning the body well. The mouth of the grave was covered with a large flat stone, and the earth dug out of the grave thrown over it. The men who covered the grave were careful to

---

96 The ancestral world

throw in the topsoil first before the red earth to form a mound. The *tsinza* players moved to the front of the deceased's room and performed *bathla mshi* (mourners' dance). The tune played for this dance was interpreted to me in the following way:

1. Wayo... wayo...
   Oh... oh...
2. Aya... wayo
   Oh no... oh...
3. Wayo... mburu a tuwa ni
   Oh... let us mourn him
4. Aya... wayo
   Oh no... oh

As this dance was performed, many shed tears profusely. Nganjiwa explained that:

> "Now that the corpse has been buried, the wives, children, relatives and friends of the deceased must express their grief by crying to show what a great loss that has occurred to them... They do this in realization of the fact that they would never physically see the deceased again. Moreover, the *Mambula* of the deceased is watching everything happening. It is, therefore, necessary that they mourn by crying or yelling; otherwise the *Mambula* becomes angry and bad luck to the family." (Nganjiwa, personal communication, 2004)

The process of the funeral for the burial day of Kida Kanti ended in the evening with most of the mourners dispersing to their various homes leaving behind only close relations. Nothing specific with regards to other rites to follow the burial was made public with the exception of making it known when the *Kuri tuwa* (the final mourning) would take place. Apparently, it occurred to me that this was so because none of Kanti's children, being Christians by religion,[97] would want to be associated with the Bura indigenous funeral rites accorded by their father. However, several months later when I went to observe the *Kuri tuwa*, it was made known to me that some rites did take place after the burial, but only very few people participated. I was made to understand that the rites were performed by Kanti's associates who are still practicing the Bura indigenous religion. Some of these associates, whom I located, were unwilling to divulge what occurred at the rites. They were nonetheless quick to point out to me that *tsinza* music was not part of those rites.

The *kuri tuwa* rites were, however, different. It was open to people and many gathered. It took place seven months after the burial. The rites start-

---

97   Christianity preaches against such practices.

ed in the afternoon of the day selected for the ceremony. All of Kanti's in-laws, and many of his relations brought animals—some rams and others goats—and presented it to the elders of his clan who were seated in front of his room. Apart from the animals, cooked food and Coca-Cola soft drinks were brought and presented on behalf of the in-laws by many of their relations. After the presentations, a ram was slaughtered beside Kanti's grave and the ram's blood was sprinkled over it.

Soon after this, the playing of *tsinza* music commenced, accompanied by a single *Ganga* (Drum) this time around. Many *tsinza* players came along with their instruments. Fifteen of them participated, including both the old and young players. They sat in a row with the leader sitting on a stool directly on top of Kanti's grave. Some of the *tsinza* musicians sat to his right-hand side while others to the left. As they performed the first tune, *para*, an old woman brought out Kanti's *Hyel kir*, personal god, from his room. She was completely covered with an indigo-dyed Bura cloth called *gabaka*. The *Hyel kir* was placed inside a calabash with some cotton wool placed around it. The woman carried it under the cover of the cloth wrapped around her. Amidst dancing to the tune being played by the musicians, the woman accompanied by several people in a procession, moved the *Hyel kir* outside the compound and placed it on the left side of the compound's entrance. As the procession moved, cotton wool and sesame seeds[98] were tossed into the air by some of the women as they danced. Sesame seeds and cotton wool, being key materials for all Bura rituals, were in this case meant to appease the *Hyel kir* to go in peace now that its owner is no longer alive.

The drum beat accompanying the *tsinza* ceased as soon as the *Hyel kir* was taken out of Kanti's room and then out of the compound completely. The *tsinza* music, however, continued. The tune played for the removal of the *Hyel kir* was *para*. This was the same as the tune played while the corpse of Kanti was being taken to the grave for burial as described above. Nganjiwa explained that:

> "Since the owner of the *Hyel kir* is dead, it is no longer of any relevance. It was his personal god. Nobody can take care of it as he did. It must therefore, be separated from the family... It is escorted by *para* because in the same manner the corpse was removed and buried, so also it should be removed. The removal this time not to bury it, but to discard it. But this must be done in such a way that it is not angered. Sacrifice of sesame seed and cotton is offered to appease it" (Nganjiwa, personal communication, 2004).

The *Hyel kir* personal god is a spirit embedded in a clay figurine. For the Bura, "spirits" don't die. But since it is a personal god and the owner is no

---

98 *Sesamum indicum*

longer alive, it must be discarded so that it also begins its journey to the land of the spirits.

After the *Hyel kir* was removed, the *para* tune was played for some time before the musicians switched to tunes that Nganjiwa explained were to entertain the guests at the gathering as they kept vigil late into the night. However, in all the tunes performed for the night, the deceased's good deeds during his life were recounted. In one of the tunes played during the night, "*mwar wa ndzi wa,*"[99] death was considered inevitable. As such, Kanti's family and associates are required by the tune to cease mourning and return to their normal lives. After all, he lived a good life so whether or not he is around, life must continue.

Other tunes played at the occasion included: *Waksha–Waksha, Tsa Bdla and Timbil Kum.* These tunes were all played to entertain the guest at the ceremony. As the music was played some of the guest engaged in dancing. The dances for all the three tunes were vigorous, as it requires the shaking of all parts of the body. Early in the morning, all the guests dispersed for their respective homes, leaving behind members of the family and some close relatives.

Kanti's funeral differs in several ways with what my informants narrated to me as the "standard" Bura funeral. For example, I observed in particular that the rite of up-rooting the *gilam* drinking water pot and the smashing of the deceased's *kuwga diva* before the seated corpse after the *kukula* dance did not take place. This reinforces what I stated earlier, that there is no such "standard" funeral. However, my goal of observing how the *tsinza* is used in Bura funerals was achieved by observing Kanti's funeral.

6.4 Tsinza as a Medium of Communication

As I reflect on the case study of Kanti's funeral that I have presented above, and try to understand the significance of the *tsinza* in Bura funerals, the question that comes to my mind is: why is it that the people do not express their sentiment of social bonding verbally and directly to the soul *mambula* of a deceased member of their society, but rather chose the *tsinza* as the medium of doing that? It is apparent from the repertoire of Bura funerals that the living members of the society choose to express the sentiments of social bounding with a deceased member of their society through the *tsinza*. The instrument is at the centre of the rites performed at funerals and plays the key role of facilitating the "communication" between the living and the dead as the *mambula* of the later is disentangled gradually from the former. The rites of the disposal of the body of the deceased, and indeed all

99 Translates as "neither gone nor around".

the other associating rites that follow at Bura funerals, are all centered on appeasing the *mambula* (soul) of the deceased, which does not depart to the ancestral world immediately after death, but hovers around in the trees of the compounds to see whether the appropriate rites are performed or not. At this stage, the *mambula* is in a marginal or liminal state (van Gennep 1960, Turner 1986) and must be reincorporated into the culturally defined roles and statuses of the society.[100]

For the process of this reincorporation, the Bura do not "communicate verbally" and "directly" to a deceased member of their society, but rather do so through the *tsinza*, an instrument that from all the legends concerning its origin is portrayed as coming from "non-natural characters." In one of the legends, first it was a dream leading to the creation of fire, which in turn led to the production of a hoe—an important tool for the largely agrarian Bura society. With the advent of the hoe, crops were cultivated and a bumper harvest was recorded. To celebrate the abundant harvest, a search for a means of doing it resulted in the "accidental" discovery of the *tsinza*. In another legend, the instrument was "stolen" from *Cicu,* one of the Bura spirit types (cf. Chapter 4). In the perception of the Bura, all the "characters" in the legends are "non-natural" and are considered to be "intermediaries" between them and an unknown "force," whom they have termed as *Hyel,* god. In the Bura worldview, *Hyel* cannot be reached directly, but only through an intermediary *haptu* (also one of the Bura spirit types). Each compound had a *haptu* shrine and each village had a common one, both an important centre for worship through which protection from danger was sought from *Hyel.*

It appears that the concept of an "intermediary" seems to be a strong aspect of the Bura worldview. The people seem to employ a "mediator" in their interactions with "non-natural beings," which are perceived to possess "supernatural powers" but live far away from them. A typical example is the belief in *Hyel,* a being considered to be "powerful" but far away from the direct reach of the people. Perhaps the Bura story about the origin of death itself illustrates this perception of the people. In the story, the failure of a certain "character" sent to make an enquiry from *Hyel* on what to do with a dead member of their society played a role that led to the people finding appropriate funeral rites for deceased members of their society. I present the story as narrated to me by one of my informants to support my argument that the Bura people seem to always employ a "mediator" in "communicating" with unseen "non-natural beings" that pervade their worldview. As a

---

100 The general structure underlying a great variety of ritual behaviour relates to the social function of recruiting and incorporating individuals that mature, age, and die into a fixed system of culturally defined roles and statuses. This function is made necessary by the fact that society outlasts the individuals that comprise it (Van Gennep, 1960).

member of the Bura society, I have also heard this story about the origin of death as a child from my grandparents. The story is as follows:

The Bura attribute the origin of death to the lizard. According to the Bura people, there was no such thing as death when *Hyel* (God) created the world. There was no disease and no crying.

One day, however, a man fell ill and died. Nobody knew what to do with him. The people around him decided that they would ask *Hyel* what to do with him. A worm, *Kulamya*, was summoned and sent to go and tell *Hyel* that a man had died, and ask *Hyel* what to do with him.

The worm went to *Hyel* and reported the incident. *Hyel* asked *Kulamya* to go and tell the people to take the corpse and hang it up in the fork of a tree and throw *macikil* (mush) at it until it came back to life. When it came back to life, no one else would ever die. The worm started back to report to the people who had been waiting. Unknowingly to *Kulamya*, a lizard, named *Agadzagadza*, over-heard his discussion with *Hyel*. *Agadzagadza* wanted to deceive. He ran very hard. When he reached the village, he said, "The worm cannot go fast, so *Hyel* sent me." *Hyel* said that I should tell you to dig a pit and wrap the corpse in cloth and put it inside. After having put it, you should fill the pit with the earth you dug out of it. The people did as *Agadzagadza* told them.

As they threw the last heap of earth onto the pit, *Kulamya* arrived. The people scolded him and demanded to know why he had not come back faster. "If the lizard had not come and told us what *Hyel* said we should do, we would still be waiting for you." said the people. *Kulamya* said, "Who sent him? You have taken his word and you have done what he said, but it is not what *Hyel* said you should do." *Kulamya* explained to them that what they did is different than what *Hyel* told him to be done. *Kulamya* told them that *Hyel* said, the corpse should be hung in a fork of a tree and *macikil* should be thrown at it until it came back to life. *Hyel* also said that when it came back to life, no one else would die again. But now you have buried it. You had better take it out of the pit and let us do what *Hyel* said we should do.

The men were overcome by laziness and they said to *Kulamya*, "It is because you did not come back more quickly that we have already buried the corpse." Due to laziness, the people decided to leave the corpse (Hanku, personal communication, 2004).

Having refused to do what *Hyel* had asked their ancestors to do and having followed the "lie" of *Agadzagadza*, the Bura people have, therefore, come a long way with "appropriate" funeral rites for the dead members of their society. The "appropriate" rites, though, require "communication" between a deceased's *mambula* and the living; a "communication" centered on the reincorporation of the *mambula* of a deceased member of their society who is in a liminal state. The reincorporation is of course into the next "status," that is, sending the *mambula* to the ancestral world where it is to reside with other ancestors of the Bura people. The Bura people themselves cannot define where the "ancestral world" is located. But in their perception, it is a place where the deceased members of their society go upon death and only after all the "appropriate" rites must have been performed to separate the dead from the living. In the people's perception, the "ancestral world" is a world that is not physically seen by the living, so it is also considered a "non-natural factor". Therefore, in order to "communicate" with a *mambula* that is in the process of being reincorporated into it requires an "intermediary". A typical case, for example, is as in the case of the Bura story of the origin of death. A scheme of "communication" derived from the story can be presented in diagram form as below:

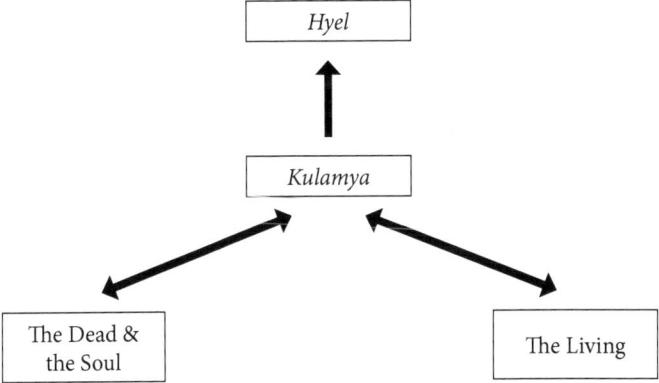

Fig. 27. Scheme of Communication in the Bura Story of Origin of Death

The *tsinza* appears to play the same role, as *kulamya* (in the middle) was required to do in the story of the origin of death - that of a "mediator". It appears in the same manner that the Bura did not approach *Hyel* directly in the story, they also do not "communicate" directly with the *mambula* of a dead member of their society that is in liminal state and undergoing the process of becoming an ancestor.[101]

Perhaps the *tsinza* is the instrument of "communication" in Bura funerals because it is also considered to come into existence from a "non-natural source" as earlier mentioned. Also, upon the death of a Bura person, it is believed that the *mambula* leaves the body and assumes the status of a "non-natural being" that can be "harmful" in many ways if not "treated" well. Any good or bad happenings in a family or a community are associ-

---

101   For deceased to become an ancestor, all the rites associated with funerals must be fully performed.

ated with a departed member of a family whose *mambula* may or may not have been treated well and, therefore, safely or not safely ensconced into the ancestral world. Care is, therefore, taken to placate the *mambula* so that it is safely ensconced into the ancestral world. Singing its praises on the *tsinza* is assumed to appease the *mambula*. In the process of singing the praises, a kind of "conversation" between the living and the dead ensues, therefore, "communication" established. A *mambula* is also assumed to "speak" back to the living through the music of the *tsinza*. A scheme of the "communication process between the living and the dead can also be presented as below:

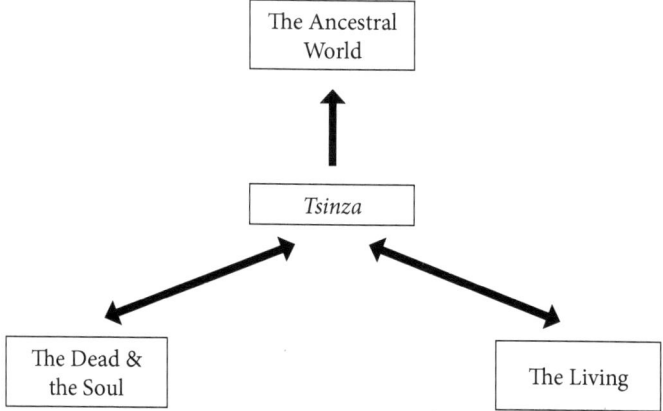

Fig. 28. Scheme of Communication through *Tsinza* at Bura Funerals

This looks similar to the scheme of "communication" illustrated earlier for the story of origin of death. Right in the middle of the "communication" between the living, the dead and soul, and the ancestral world, is the *tsinza*. The living members of the society who are required to perform the appropriate rites to ensconce the dead whose *mambula* is in a liminal state and can be "harmful" if not treated well, do not "speak" directly with it. Similarly, the dead, whose *mambula* has become "invincible" to the living and observes whether it is treated well, does not speak directly to the living either. Rather, the sentiment of social bonds between the living and the dead is expressed through the music of the *tsinza*. The living "speak" to the dead through the *tsinza*, just as the dead speaks to the living through the *tsinza*. The ultimate goal of "communicating" with each other is for the living to "safely" separate the dead from themselves and this can only be achieved, in the Bura worldview, through the *tsinza*.

As observed in the case study of Kanti's funeral, the "communication" started right with the music that announces his death. The song about *kaka*

grandfather, symbolically expresses how "important" Kanti had been to especially his grandchildren and other children of the community, who also
joined in singing it. Soon after the first tune, the *mambula* of the deceased
"announces" its "departure" to the brothers, sisters, wives and his "boss"
through the second tune played by the *tsinza* player. This demonstrates a
clear case of "communication". The living "spoke" first and the *mambula*
responded by "announcing" to all his journey "home."

Each step of the rite was accompanied by music, which if symbolically interpreted, is a "communication" between the living and the dead. In
some of the songs, certain animals are used to express some situations and
the character of Kanti as well. For example, the death of Kanti was linked
to *Duku* (eagle). In the perception of the Bura, *Duku* is a "swift" bird of
"strength" and, it is the only "force" that is capable of snatching a loved one
from them through death. Death is considered as something that happens
"swiftly," otherwise, if they have their way, they would stop it. Singing such
a song at a funeral is an expression of the affection the living members of a
society have for a departed member. Similarly, a song comparing Kanti to
Hwalang, a specie of snake not considered poisonous and, therefore, not
harmful, was sung as part of the repertoire at his funeral. The song symbolically expresses how "peaceful" Kanti had been while alive. This is considered as "speaking good" and "praising" the character of Kanti. Such tunes
are required to safely establish the *mambula* of a deceased in the ancestral
world. *Tsinza* music is what the Bura use to express such sentiments of social bonds to the deceased members of their society.

6.5 Conclusion

The information presented in this chapter on the Bura funeral is, like the
chapter on the Bura *tsinza,* heavily drawn from oral history. However, my
participation in Kanti's funeral afforded me the opportunity to observe and
collect first hand information on indigenous funeral practices of the people.
Also, it granted me a better understanding of what the Bura themselves
described to me in several interviews as their indigenous funeral rites.
Through my participation, however, I observed and noted some differences
between what was narrated to me by my informants and what I witnessed.
The differences observed might not be unrelated to my comment at the beginning of the section describing Bura funerals that there is no such thing
as a "standard" funeral in any given society.[102] Funerals do vary in the scale
of the rites performed and in many other ways. However, it is also important to note that Kanti's funeral took place not too long ago, and at a time

---

102 cf. page 115.

when the Bura society had undergone some influences of "modernity". What my informants described for me was a recollection of what in the people's "memory" was the rites performed at Bura funerals. What I observed is what took place recently; thus, there are bound to be differences.

What I have dealt with so far in this and in the previous chapters can be considered as what Bielawski (1985: 10) has termed "past history". The previous chapters, therefore, mainly dwelled on the "past history" of Bura society. "Past history" in the sense that the Bura have also encountered what Bielawski termed as "immediate past history". I shall at this point turn to the "immediate past history" of the Bura. In the next chapters, I will consider the introduction of Christianity in Bura land and the impact it has had on the indigenous practices of the people. The next chapter will be followed by one on the *tsinza* in its contemporary context. This is to examine how the "immediate past history" has impacted the traditional context of use of the *tsinza*, and how it has likely created a "new culture" through its continual use amongst the people.

7 The Introduction of Christianity to Bura Land

7.1 Introduction

One major event that caused a significant shift in Bura history was the commencement of missionary work in the area in 1923 by the Church of the Brethren Mission. Ever since the contact of the Bura people with the missionaries, many indigenous practices were either completely abandoned or underwent significant changes. The educational and health care system introduced by the missionaries suddenly offered a new way of life to the people. This chapter discusses the introduction of Christianity to Bura land, and its impact on the indigenous practices of the people.

7.2 The Beginning of Mission Work

Missionary interest and propaganda in the northeastern part of Nigeria may have begun before the 18th century, but it was not until the second half of the 19th century that Christian bodies in Britain, United States, Canada and Italy expressed their desire to begin missionary work in the area. By 1881, the American Board of Commission for Foreign Mission indicated the wish to introduce Christianity in the Yola district (Ayandele, 1966: 503), but interest waned and the idea was dropped at least for the mean time. Although a number of areas were considered, the answer finally came through the missionary explorer, Dr. H.K.W. Kumm, then a secretary of the Sudan United Mission (S.U.M.). Having explored some parts of Adamawa and Borno, he found out that these areas had a population of well over half a million of non-Moslems (Kulp, 1954:1), and was a challenging field for missionary efforts.

In October 1916, Kumm went on a speaking tour of the American Church Colleges. He delivered a lecture on Africa at Manchester College. This was followed by a special plea to the Church of the Brethren to help build a chain of missions across Africa to stem the tide of Islamic invasion and to help win Central Africa for Christianity (Moyer, 1931: 190). His plea appealed to seven students who formed a prayer band in the 'interest' of Africa, and volunteered to open up mission fields. Three years later, in 1919, the first request for a mission field was made at the Peter Becker Bicentennial Conference, Winona Lake, Indiana. By September 1922, The General Mission Board had selected Northern Nigeria as its probable mission field. Reverend and Mrs. Harold Stover Kulp of Pennsylvania and Reverend and

Mrs. Albert D. Helser of Ohio were appointed as an Investigation Commission. It was arranged that the two men should leave their wives behind before a definite site had been located.

One of the major factors that influenced the Church of the Brethren Mission to give first Priority to Northern Nigeria for its probable mission field was a report titled, "Education Committee to Africa," by Thomas Jesse Jones, Director of the Phelps-Stokes Fund (Moyer, 1931: 191). The Phelps-Stokes Fund had been established for educational purposes in the 'interest of Negroes in Africa and United States' according to the provisions of the will of Miss Caroline Phelps-Stokes. In 1920 to 1921, a commission was sent to West and South Africa under the auspices of this fund at the request of American Missionary Societies who wanted a survey report before they developed their educational program for post-war Africa. The general scope and objectives of the commission were "to study the educational needs of Africa, especially those pertaining to hygienic, economic, social and religious conditions of the native people." (Baldwin, 1973:65)

Jones' report further stated that Northern Nigeria offered unlimited opportunities for educational development. The government at the time of the commission's visit was building a teacher-training institution among the Moslem peoples of the North West. The government and the mission agreed that another equally well-equipped school should be established in the North East. As the government could not undertake this responsibility, it was further agreed that Christian Missions should undertake the task. The Church of the Brethren Mission in America seized this opportunity, and on December 29, 1922, the investigation commission arrived in Nigeria with letters of introduction from J. H. Oldham, Secretary of the International Missionary Council; and with copies of Jones' 'Education in Africa' in hand, they presented themselves to the Governor, Sir Hugh Clifford in Lagos. A Lagos paper, the *Nigerian Pioneer* from the 5th of January, 1923 noted:

> "You perhaps already know that partly as an outcome of the Phelps-Stokes Educational Commission which visited Nigeria in 1920–21, there have arrived in Lagos on their way to Bornu two American gentlemen, Messrs. Helser and Kulp, as an investigation commission to Nigeria under the auspices of the General Mission Board of the Church of the Brethren to found an industrial institution among the pagans of the north" (cited from Helser, 1926:23).

After consultations with other missionary bodies and the colonial government in Lagos and Kaduna, Messrs. Helser and Kulp were directed to open a mission field, on behalf of the Church of the Brethren, in the southern part of Borno Province, in the district of Biu, which had a non-Moslem population of more than two hundred thousand (Kulp, 1954:3)

Upon the arrival of Helser and Kulp to Biu, the capital[103] of the Bura people on February 12, 1923, Major Frank Edgar, the District Officer of the Division (D.O.), granted them hospitality. But upon making a request to begin work at Yimir Pilasar, a small hamlet of about one and half kilometers west of Biu, they ran into opposition from the Emir, Mai Ali Dogo, and a Moslem. According to the Emir, Biu already had a small Moslem population (mostly the Pabir, Hausa traders, and the settled Fulani). Therefore, acceptance of missionary presence in the area was seen as a threat to Islam and had to be resisted. Edgar, not wanting to create a problem between himself and the Emir, refused permission. He insisted that the matter be taken up with the Resident, H. R. Palmer, in Maiduguri. According to him, this was in keeping with the policy of the colonial government. Naturally, the missionaries interpreted the D.O.'s action as favoring Islam over Christianity. Unbeknownst to the missionaries, the D.O., in his report to the Resident, strongly opposed the missionary presence in Biu Division. Kulp later wrote about the Resident's opposition of their presence:

"It happened that the Resident, although an able administrator, belonged to the group who opposed missions on the ground of policy. That is, he favoured all people coming under the Moslem emirs and felt the coming of Christian missions was not at that time a desirable step in the development of the country. He took the objection of the local chief at Biu as sufficient reason for advising against our application being granted. We had, however, the written statement of the governor that it was not the government policy to prohibit missions even though the paramount chief was a Moslem if the mass of the people was still pagan" (Kulp, 1968:70)

The Resident did, however, grant permission to settle at Garkida, 56 kilometers away from Biu, the Emir's headquarters. On March 8, 1923, the investigation had reached Garkida, and Helser wrote:

"Finally we have reached the place where we have been given the right to build... We are just here on good behaviour, because the old Borno Province has always been closed to missions. We pray that this may be an entrance into the hearts of 200,000 people speaking the Bura language. These are practically all pagan and seem open to teaching" (cited from Moyer, 1931:192).

In Garkida, the coming of the missionaries was received with mixed feelings. To many of the people, this was the first time they had contact with 'the white man'. Some had heard or witnessed how 'the white man' imposed

---

103 The Bura people that had lived previously under a non-centralised political system were subjected under the Pabir Emir of Biu by the colonial government.

his rule over the area.[104] It was then curious that 'the white man' now wanted to live amongst them. There was also a reaction from the minority Moslem Fulani and Hausa traders who saw the missionaries as "infidels," and thus became skeptical of their presence in Garkida. The choice of a site for a permanent residential area of the missionaries also increased the skepticism of the people. After spending the first few days in the Garkida rest house, they located a permanent residential site at *Kufa – tuzhakuma* (Lake of Small Pox) where the mission buildings still stand today. *Kufa – tuzhakuma* was a place where spirits were believed to have lived, and it was strongly believed that when the missionaries settled there, the spirits would kill them. Looking at it now, the pioneer missionaries might have chosen this site because it was, and still is, the best-elevated area in Garkida. This hilly area was not only the least mosquito-infested, but also offered the missionaries the much needed privacy to which they might have been accustomed to in the West.

Nine days after their arrival in Garkida, they had the groundbreaking service for the first mission building on March 17, 1923 (...). This date marked the establishment of the Church of the Brethren Mission in Bura land in particular, and in Nigeria in general.

7.3 Impact of the Missionaries on Bura Land

There are many activities, which a missionary undertakes. She or he must preach the word of God, teach at school, make roads, write books, attend to the sick—but she or he must not lose the passion for converts (considered "lost" souls)—to the new religion, nor must she or he forget that everything she or he does has the ultimate aim of bringing souls to Christ (Kulp, 1968: 147, Ronk, 1971: 112). Thus, the missionaries in Bura land considered one of their most important tasks to bring the "lost" and "heathen" souls to Christ. In compliance with this cardinal objective, they quickly established churches, schools and medical facilities in the area. These institutions provided them a base from which to preach the word of God.

The impact of the American missionaries is similar to that of the colonial administration, in that they both represented an intrusion into the Bura way of life. It impacted upon the social, economic and political world of the people. The missionaries sought the creation of a completely new social order, which wiped out most of the customs and institutions of the Bura people. They condemned completely what they saw of the traditional society, and set up requirements for becoming accepted in the newly established Christian community. This meant for the people an abandonment of many of the social customs basic to the fabrics of their everyday lives.

---

104 The encounter with British colonialists.

Many of the missionaries brought their family members and lived permanently in places where mission fields were established. They lived as much as possible to their Western standards and imported as much as possible their social framework into the communities where they settled. As a result of their interaction with the people, their theological approach, marriage system, burial customs (a few died soon after arrival) came to be considered as the best by their converts. This consequently fostered processes of imitation, emulation and 'Americanization.'

The missionaries were as well fired with idealism of faith to which they attributed the progresses in technological achievement and moral enlightenment of their home countries. They considered that the indigenous customs and institutions did not comprise any wisdom of value (Ayandele, 1966:4). This ethnocentrism led them to strive for the replacement of the traditional scheme of things with a totally Americanized "Christian Civilization."

In this endeavor, one of the greatest impacts of the American missionaries on Bura land was the replacement of the Bura traditional religion with the new Christian faith. The basis for conversion to the new faith emphasized the "exalted individual" (Ayandele, 1966: 330). For the missionary, one must build and maintain his or her own personal faith and relationship with God. The individual, and not the family, group, clan or tribe must make the decision. Consequently, individuals and not social units were converted. This cultural confrontation was a direct disruption of the indigenous communal Bura tribal solidarity[105]. Every member of the group, village or tribe was a unit of an entity, controlled by a code of duties, taboos and rights on which the faithful performance of every individual depended. It was only as a unit in the entity that they must think, believe and act. They had to submit to the collective will and authority of the community in this manner so as to enable them and the community to exist.

When the missionaries converted the individual, they removed a unit from the entity and thereby undermined the monolithic structure of the society. The converts not only imbibed a new set of religious beliefs, but also began to nurse 'alien' ideas, economic ambitions and political aspirations of their own, detrimental to the welfare and the solidarity of the community. This was particularly true in the first decade of missionary work in Garkida when the group of Christian converts was very small and the sense of identity in the community was "nebulous" (Baldwin, 1973: 139) due to a 'Western' if not necessarily Christian emphasis on individualism.

Since the Bura culture was basically a religious culture and its customs and behavior were so closely tied to religious beliefs, the missionaries in attempting to convert the people to a new way of life struck at the core of the old patterns. A typical example of this was in the area of music. Before

---

105 The was no individuality in traditional Bura society.

the introduction of Christianity in the area, music played a central role in all rituals, especially funerals. The music of the *tsinza* in particular, was a very important component of indigenous funerals. But with the coming of Christianity, converts were not permitted to dance to any form of music, even at Christian occasions. Dancing to traditional music, therefore, seemed even more 'evil' since it was often a part of rituals and ceremonies involving supplications to the spirits (*shatan*). Dancing to the music of the *tsinza*, which still today is closely associated with Bura identity, became the most affected by the stand of the missionaries against any form of dancing. This had a significant impact on the use of the *tsinza* amongst the people. Many of the converts turned their backs on an instrument closely associated with their identity leading to the decline of its use in the society.[106] Questions about the instrument, especially by children, were never answered directly by adults, many of whom had long converted to Christianity.

Furthermore, tunes that were commonly sung by the Bura singers were not used in Christian services. Instead, the missionaries set Bura words to hymnal tunes from the hymnbook brought from America, and taught these so that they would become part of Christian worship. It was not until the early sixties that traditional tunes were commonly used in Christian settings as the indigenous song leaders proposed new words for them, which they often composed on the spot.

To the best of my knowledge, there exists no substantial written evidence to show why and how the use of traditional tunes became acceptable in Christian worship by the missionaries. However, it appears the process of the acceptance took place over a long period of time. From Garkida, the missionaries expanded to other areas of Bura land. They got permission to open mission stations in places that they were previously forbidden to operate in.[107] One example of such a mission station was the one at Marama, opened in 1931. With the opening of more stations, the missionaries had to make certain crucial decisions. According to the accounts of one of the missionaries, Irene Bittinger, who lived in Garkida and Marama in the 1930s, "... some decisions had to be made at this time: Do the missionaries make the rules? Set the goals? Take the leadership? What is the position of the Nigerian? How long should the missionary remain? Should the Nigerian "take charge"? When? How soon?"(Bittinger 2005:22). These questions demonstrate the dilemma of the missionaries at that moment. Perhaps, subsequent answers to some of these questions as witnessed by developments in the mission work for years to follow, explain among other things, why traditional songs substituted with new words became acceptable in Christian

---

106 The teaching of the missionaries on the indigenous practices of the people as "evil" caused many to no longer take part in such practices.

107 Permission from the colonial government of the period.

worship. By the 1960s, many Bura priests had been ordained and assumed responsibilities for some of the churches.[108] It would not, therefore, be out of place to speculate that the attitude of such priests towards traditional songs with new words being used in worship would have been different from those of the American missionaries. Being part and parcel of the tradition themselves, they might not have seen anything wrong with singing such songs with new words, substituting the original. After all, Bittinger suggests that "[i]t was our goal to have the Nigerians 'take on' and 'take over' the 'building and growth' of the church to have it be 'their' church, as completely and rapidly as possible" (Bittinger 2005: 21). Perhaps this "goal" paved the way for the use of traditional songs in church worship. However, the problem of dancing and the use of indigenous musical instruments continued unresolved (Baldwin, 1973:141) for quite some time.

On June 22, 1972, the local church became independent from the Church of Brethren Mission in America (CBM). It changed its name to *Ekklisiyar Yan'uwa a Nigeria* (EYN), which means "the Church of the Brethren in Nigeria". Even with the church becoming independent, the problem of dancing and the use of indigenous musical instruments persisted in the first few years. Many of the missionaries remained and continued to play key roles in the running of the affairs of the church. This, however, did not stop some indigenous instruments, particularly the *tsinza*, from finding their way into the church. Those converts that can play the instrument began playing it as accompaniment to the traditional tunes commonly used in Christian settings.

Again, to the best of my knowledge, there is no clear-cut reason as to why indigenous instruments were permitted into the church after it had become independent. But it is true that no one can point to any written document produced by the American missionaries forbidding the use of traditional instruments in the church. In discussions held with some serving and retired indigenous priests of the church (Reverends Usman Lima, Mamadu Kwaya, Samuel Shinggu), none of them seemed to be aware of any written law that traditional instruments should not be used in the church. According to them, the missionaries simply disapproved of dancing and the use of traditional instruments because they were associated with traditional beliefs, and therefore, considered "evil" and not appropriate to be used in Christian worship.

Perhaps, one of the reasons why indigenous instruments, especially the *tsinza*, found their way into the church was that the converts realised that nothing could stop them from using their traditional instruments in the church so long as they were used in a 'Christian' context. Moreover, some of the converts at that time in the course of their travels to big cities had come

---

108 A bible training school was opened soon after the commencement of missionary activities in Bura land.

into contact with other churches established by other missionary groups and had seen indigenous instruments being used. There were other missionary groups who established churches in some parts of Nigeria much earlier than in Bura land. In such churches, women singing groups commonly used traditional musical instruments, especially clay pots of different sizes, with origins from the Igbo ethnic group of southeast Nigeria. This must have impacted the Bura converts, making them see that nothing was in fact "wrong" with using indigenous instruments in the church.

Besides the activities of the missionaries wiping out many of the customs and institutions of the Bura people, many in the society consider their impact in the areas of Western education and medicine as immeasurable. By building schools in the area they certainly did introduce Western education in Bura land for the first time.[109] The Mission's educational policy of a self-supporting basis provided for a vast array of occupational possibilities for the people. Many alumni of the mission schools took to professional careers that had social status and dignity in colonial and post-colonial Nigeria, such as in education, medicine, politics and business. For example, the Garkida mission schools in this respect subsequently produced the first Northern Nigerian pilot, the first woman medical doctor in Borno State, the first Bura member of Nigeria's olympic games team in 1948 (Eikenbery 1959: 16), and the first Bura member of the Northern Nigeria House of Assembly and Legislative Council.

Thus, one of the most important results of the missionary's endeavor in the field of education was the emergence of the Bura elites who were educated not only in Western literacy skills and techniques, but also in Western ways of thinking. However, this also had a negative effect on the society. It greatly impacted individuals, resulting in a change in the way some indigenous practices were perceived. Many of the elites have abandoned some practices that they consider not to conform to the "learned" Western way of thinking.

7.4 Conclusion

This chapter largely dealt with the introduction of Christianity in Bura land and the effect it had on the indigenous practices of the people in the region. The aspect of dancing to traditional music was particularly singled out amongst the many other practices that the religion impacted. It is singled out because my thesis' principal concern is the Bura xylophone *tsinza*, an instrument closely associated with Bura identity, but which was forbidden for use in Christian activities for a period of many years. This was because

---

109 There was no school in Bura land before the commencement of missionary work.

of the conception of the missionaries that the instrument was "evil," since it was associated with indigenous rituals. While it might be true that the missionaries' activities impacted positively in certain aspects of the way of life of the people, in some other aspects the impact could be seen as negative. The adoption of Christianity by some of the people meant that control of indigenous customs and restrictions was lessened, due to some of the factors discussed in this chapter. The *tsinza* tradition, which before the introduction of Christianity played a key role in funerals, is one of those indigenous customs that was very much affected by the societal control of the missionaries and the people's embrace of a new religion that significantly changed their worldview. The instrument was gradually adopted for use in the church after a period of non-acceptance. However, the meanings associated with it changed in the Christian context and indeed in many other occasions where it is used in contemporary times.

The next chapter discusses the *tsinza* in its contemporary context. The instrument is still used in present day Bura society. However, "new" contexts of use seem to have emerged as a result of the "immediate past history" of the people.

8 The *Tsinza* in its Contemporary Context

8.1 Introduction

The focus of this chapter is on the significance of the *tsinza* in contemporary Bura society. The traditional context of *tsinza* performance, as discussed in Chapter 6 of this study, has significantly changed and is gradually disappearing.[110] This is largely due to the adoption of Christianity as a new religion by many of the people as discussed in the preceding chapter. The adoption of a new religion changed the attitude of the Bura converts towards many of their indigenous cultural practices. However, "new" contexts of use of the instrument seem to have emerged and appear to be keeping *tsinza* performance a lively art amongst the people. It is the "new" context of use that this chapter seeks to explore in order to understand why and in what ways the Bura maintain xylophone music and performance even though the traditional context of performance is gradually disappearing. While it is true that the instrument is still considered a "funeral instrument" by the non-Christianized Bura, it is used in contemporary times in connection with other musical occasions, including Christian-related ones, despite the initial stance of the missionaries who brought Christianity to the area (cf. Chapter 4). The instrument could be seen as having moved from being originally a funeral instrument as emphasized by its older musicians, to other uses as carried out by the younger *tsinza* players.

The strategy in this chapter is, therefore, to discuss the contemporary context of use of the instrument in Bura musical occasions. I will rely on my experience as a member of Bura society, born and bred in Bura land, and as a scholar. The data I present here in this chapter is a result of participant observation and other aspects of field research which have allowed me to deepen and widen my knowledge of the contemporary role of the tsinza in Bura land.

8.2 Bura Occasions of Musical Activities

Like in so many other African languages, Bura does not have a specific word for music. Expressions like "song" or "dance" are used to determine the wide range of musical performances, which are closely linked to the cycles of life and the seasons, as well as various other social activities. Alan P. Merriam notes that in Africa, a song:

---

110   There are fewer funerals carried out in the indigenous way in present day Bura society.

... tends to be tied to the socio-cultural events for which it is created, without the event the music is not produced... songs are not thought of as independent and separable units with distinctive titles but rather as sound entities which are identified as a part of the interrelated set of activities that constitute an occasion. While westerners tend to stress composer and song title, Africans stress the type of song and the situation of which it is a part (Merriam 1982: 140).

However, not all social activities in Bura land require music. The situation appears to be similar to what J.H. Kwabena Nketia observes with regard to Ghanaian folk music:

Not all activities or all occasions on which particular activities take place are associated with music. A beer festival or a procession may, in one and the same society, be traditionally linked with music, while drinking in the home or walking by individuals may not. A millet beer (*pitoo*) bar may be a place for making music, while the shrine of ... priest of the land, may not. This is to say a distinction is maintained between musical events and non-musical events (Nketia 1963: 4-5)

In a study of Bura folk's songs, Zainab Haruna (1998) categorizes Bura social activities into formal and informal occasions. She notes that:

... occasion could be formal. This means that they are well-planned and organised social events such as naming ceremonies, wedding ceremonies, funeral ceremonies and annual festivals... or the occasion could be informal, that is, neither planned nor organised, and might include such activities as doing a solitary work, putting child to sleep or drinking beer at a pub (Haruna 1998: iv –v).

For the purpose of this study, I will categorize Bura occasions for musical performance into official/ritual and private occasions. Official/ritual occasions would include such events as: *kuri tuwa* (final rites of a funeral); *lita zibil/bulikur* (separating a twin from the "twin world"); *Bur'kau* (communal grinding of sorghum into flour); *Bar kira kuhyi* (installation of a new chief); *Mbal tsuha laku* (beer feast for clearing of footpaths); Christmas and Easter celebrations, Moslem festivals such as *Eid-al-fitr* (end of Ramadan) and *Eid-al-adha* (feast of the sacrifice) celebrations. Meanwhile, private occasions include: *kildzi/lausa* (wedding); *kukula* (clearing of new farmland); and *Vavh thlim* (naming ceremony of a new born baby). Music is always part of these occasions; and an occasion determines which type of music and instrument are to be used. Instruments can be used either as solo or in an ensemble.

Some of the occasions mentioned above have their roots in rituals of traditional Bura society while occasions like Christmas, Easter and the Moslem celebrations came into being with the adoption of Christianity and Islam by some Bura people. As discussed in Chapter 6 of this study, the *tsinza* is a key instrument in indigenous Bura funerals. *Lita zibil* or *bulikur* (twin's rites) is a rite performed by the Bura to appease the 'spirits' thought to be associated with twins.[111] For a twin to be healthy, to behave 'normally', or even to be successfully married or in other life endeavors, the Bura believe that at one point in his or her life, she or he must be separated from the 'spirit world.' Music is part of the many other rites required to separate twins from the 'spirit world' at such an occasion. For this event, *tsinza* is not used, but rather a *gulum* player who specializes in performing music for these rituals provides the music.

Bur'kau (communal grinding of sorghum into flour), was a musical occasion that took place in all Bura communities before the introduction of industrial grinding machines into the area in the early 1960s. Prior to the introduction of the machines, stone grinding mills were used to grind sorghum—the main staple of the Bura people—into flour used in preparing mush that is eaten with various kinds of soups. Girls from 18 to 22 years of age take part in such communal ritual-grinding occasions. Each of the girls brings sorghum from their compounds to grind to the rhythm of music played by a *gulum* or *yakandi* player.

Bar kira kuhyi, the installation of a chief, is a colonial invention.[112] Before the advent of colonialism, the Bura political organization lacked leaders or hierarchies (cf. Chapter 3), therefore, such an occasion could not have existed before the introduction of colonialism in the area. However, in contemporary Bura society, chiefs are now installed and the occasion is celebrated with various musical performances, including the *tsinza*.

Mbal tsuha laku (beer feast for clearing of footpaths) is an annual festival that takes place in Bura communities. In involves ceremonial clearing of all footpaths within a community towards the end of the rainy season (September/October), and shortly before the harvest of crops planted in the year (November/December). The festival is celebrated with musical performances as well, of which the *tsinza* also plays a significant role in contemporary Bura society.

The private occasions, which include *Kukula* (clearing of a new farmland), *Kildzi/Lausa* (wedding), and *Vah thlim* (naming ceremony of a new born baby), are occasions whose planning and execution is left up to the individual concerned (i.e. deciding on what kind of music to be performed for the celebration, which ensemble to invite, and so on). In the case of

---

111 Twins are believed to be of preternatural origin in most African societies. The Bura believe they possess powers exceeding what is natural or regular which, must be from the "spirit world".

112 In pre-colonial times, the Bura political system was acephalous (cf. Chapter 3).

Kukula, however, drum music is considered to be the most appropriate. It is believed that drum music motivates them to work harder in the clearing of a new farmland whenever they are invited for such an occasion. Interestingly though, in the repertoire of a Bura traditional funeral of an elderly person, one of the rites that takes place is the playing of a *Kukula* tune by a *tsinza* player as a corpse is rested against a granary and the farming dance performed before it (cf. Chapter 6). None of my informants could explain why drum music is the most preferred in contemporary times, even though this practice appears to have its roots in the *tsinza* tune played at traditional funeral as part of the ritual to demonstrate how successful a farmer a deceased adult man had been while alive. From a scholarly point of view, it would be plausible to link the switch from *tsinza* to drums as a result of the change in the meaning of the instrument after the people's encounter with Christianity. The *tsinza* has ceased to be viewed as an important funeral instrument by the converted Bura. In contemporary Bura society the instrument has most importantly become part of a drum ensemble referred to as a *bansuwe* group, and used as well in other contexts that may be termed 'new.'

The Christian and Moslem festivals celebrated with traditional music, for example, are 'new' occasions created by the adoption of the two religions by the people as mentioned earlier. Traditional dances especially *bansuwe*, are used in the celebration of the festivals. Indeed, the *bansuwe* dance has become the dominant dance at all Bura celebrations. However, there are still some occasions where the *tsinza* is used as a solo instrument. In particular, it has found its way into being used more and more at Christian occasions after its initial rejection by the church. Today, it has become part of the instruments used by the various choir groups of the church.[113] It is used as accompaniment to songs of the choir groups at any occasion that requires music. The most interesting of the Christian occasions in which the use of the instrument is maintained are Christian funerals. As this use of the *tsinza* is different from that in indigenous funerals, it can be said that a 'new' context of use has been created.

The *tsinza* is furthermore used as a solo instrument in *kildzi/lausa* (wedding celebrations in contemporary Bura society. This is also a 'new' context considering the fact that the instrument had been an important funeral instrument. Considering the 'new' context of use of the instrument mentioned, there is no doubt that the meaning of the *tsinza* and its music has changed significantly in Bura society. I will, therefore, discuss some of these 'new' contexts separately in order to point out the role of the instrument in contemporary Bura society.

---

113 Most churches in Bura land have more than one choir group.

8.2.1 *Bansuwe* Dance

On the whole, Bura people appear to have a repertory of 20 to 25 different dances. Apart from dances like *waksha–waksha, chara–chara,* or *kwaja–kwaja*—to mention but a few—*bansuwe* occupies a prominent position.
This is even more interesting as *bansuwe* is a comparatively new dance,
which has within a short period of time become more or less synonymous
with Bura dance. A man named Saidu Kida is believed to have invented
the dance in the mid 1960s. There are different opinions with regard to the
origin of the word *"bansuwe,"* which is not a Bura word. One version insists
that *bansuwe* refers to Mercedes Benz trucks because the dance steps consist
of an engine-like, stomping; in this case, "Benz" would have become *"bansuwe".* Another account maintains that *bansuwe* refers to anything new, referring to the way in which new farming techniques would be referred to as
bansuwe as much as would the Mercedes Benz truck at the beginning of its
appearance on Bura land.

Accordingly, Saidu Kida's dance was called *bansuwe.* The novelty of the
dance is that the dancers are turning in all four directions instead of the
usual forward and sideways movements. Apart from this obvious novelty,
bansuwe allows the dancers the widest scope of liberties leading to the development of individual dance styles.

The Bura have no recollection of the exact period during which the *tsinza* became part of a *bansuwe* ensemble, which contains *ganga, kwala, and
algaita* (see section 7.2 of this chapter). However, some of my informants
(Audu Bata, Usman Boja, Hamza Nganjiwa) were of the opinion that it became part of the ensemble after many members of the society converted to
Christianity and were prohibited by church doctrines to neither use it—as
in the case of the funeral of a family member—nor participate in its use
at traditional funerals when death occurs within a community. Whatever
the case may be, the use of the *tsinza* as part of a *bansuwe* ensemble is a
'new' context within which the instrument is used. Though it is not the
lead instrument of the group as it drops behind the drum, which is the lead
instrument, the *tsinza* player functions as the lead singer of the ensemble.
Bansuwe dances are most often accompanied by singing songs that go with
the drumming. Such songs could be songs of praise or mocking of individuals within the society (cf. Chapter 5). It is the responsibility of the *tsinza*
player to compose such songs or learn it from others.

8.2.2 *Kildzi/Lausa* (Wedding)

There are basically three forms of *kildzi/lausa* (weddings) in contemporary Bura society: traditional, Christian and Muslim. The details of the different forms of *kildzi/lausa* will not be discussed, as it is not of much interest to the discussion in this chapter. Rather, the focus of this chapter is on the use of the *tsinza* in celebrating the occasion after all the formal rites are performed.

After all the ceremonies of *lausa* are performed in the daytime, the evening and indeed the whole night of the day of the occasion are used for *hir di* (celebrations). The groom, bride and their guests spend the evening dancing to *bansuwe* music while *gulum*, *yakandi* and *tsinza* musicians entertain at night. The entertainment at night is based on a reenactment of *bur' kau*—an occasion for grinding sorghum as described above. *Bur' kau* is reenacted with women taking turns to grind rhythmically to the tune of the *tsinza*, *yakandi* or *gulum* music during a *hir di* ceremony to entertain the wedding guests. It is also an avenue for the newly married bride to symbolically display her skills in grinding sorghum into flour. Apart from entertaining the wedding guests, the practice is an opportunity for a bride to demonstrate her capabilities of being able to take care for her new home in terms of preparing meals.[114]

In times past, it was the responsibility of a *gulum* or *yakandi* player to provide the music for such an occasion. This has changed in contemporary times, and *tsinza* music is also performed at such occasions. This is also another 'new' context for the instrument. The songs played at such occasions are mainly praise songs. The *tsinza* musicians that perform at such occasions are mainly young people. However, some of the tunes they play at *hir di* are found by the older generation of players to be inappropriate for such occasions, as they consider them funeral tunes that ought not be performed out of context. It is obvious, therefore, that the younger generation of *tsinza* musicians are today playing tunes as entertainment music that was formerly played in the context of funeral rites. The question remains, however, do they consciously or unconsciously play it? Or is it that the music means different things to different generations? Quite obviously, that appears to be the case—perhaps not even only for different generations, but also for different segments of society. For example, a young *tsinza* musician, Yahaya, explained to me that:

> "… Some of the traditional tunes fit perfectly with my dance songs. I play mainly at weddings and my audience want to dance. Dancing at a funeral is different from dancing at a wedding party. So I play tunes that are danceable not minding whether they are funeral tunes. Moreover, I sing the praises of

---

114   In Bura society, preparation of meals is considered the responsibility of women.

my patrons along the tunes, and they like it very much. As long as my audience appreciates it, I play it. The whole thing is to play the music in a more 'modern', and more 'attractive' way" (Yahaya, personal communication, 2012).

Yahaya's statement is a clear indication that the younger *tsinza* players are not clinging rigidly to the old ways, but are part of a gradual change, creating something new out of the old. Thus, it could be said that contemporary wedding celebrations create one of the avenues for 'new' context for the use of the *tsinza*.

8.2.3 Christian Occasions

With the adoption of Christianity by many of the Bura, many of their traditional practices also took new forms. It appears efforts were made by the people to make some of their musical occasions adapt to the requirements of the new religion. One such occasion is the funeral, which is very important for the people because of their beliefs about death. A new aspect of funeral rites that significantly differs from the traditional one discussed in Chapter 6 of this study has come into existence. While the concept and symbolic meanings behind the rites performed at Christian funerals differ from those of traditional ones; however, certain elements of traditional practices appear to be maintained. It appears the missionaries allowed some of the traditional practices of the people to be adapted—though with some modification—in their quest to win them over to Christianity. For example, instead of a woman giving three loud screams to announce the death of a man and four for a woman, as is the traditional practice of announcing a death, the church bell is rung three times for a man and four for a woman (cf. Chapter 6). Similarly, the church also adopted a practice whereby the death of a young person is considered a sad event and as such not 'celebrated.' However, if the deceased is considered to be an elderly person that has lived a long life (50 years old and above), such a death is 'celebrated' as in the traditional case. The celebration, however, was initially devoid of the *tsinza* or any other indigenous musical instrument.

The rejection of the *tsinza*, and indeed other traditional musical instruments by the church, appears however to have been given way over a period of time, especially when the indigenous church became independent from the American church that brought Christianity to Bura land (cf. Chapter 7). Today, the *tsinza* is used at Christian funerals. Perhaps this became possible because the people themselves became educated through the educational program established by the missionaries, and can read and interpret the Bible on their own. They might have come to the realization that they did not have to give up their culture completely for the culture of the missionaries to live with them and vice versa. As a young *tsinza* player, Jerry Musa, who plays the instrument at Christian occasions, explained to me:

> ... what of the instruments mentioned in the Bible? We see illustrations or photographs of it in the Bible. Are they not from a culture? Who knows what they were originally used for before Christianity came into existence? It was a misunderstanding on part of the missionaries to label the *tsinza* and other instruments as "evil". I cannot find any where in the Bible where it is stated that people should not use their instruments to worship God (Jerry, personal communication, 2014)

The technology of construction and organology of the *tsinza* used at Christian occasions mostly remain the same as the one used in traditional musical occasions. However, more recently, the decoration of some of the *kugwa tsinza* that are used at Christian occasions is being replaced with the crucifix—the symbol of Christianity—painted in very bright colors (see fig. 29).

Fig. 29. Decoration type of some of the tsinza used in Christian context

For the purpose of this study, I will use Christian funerals as an example amongst many other Christian occasions to demonstrate how the converted Bura maintain the use of the tsinza. I will describe in detail the rites performed at Christian funerals to demonstrate how the reconciliation and integration of Bura indigenous practices with the new religious system has created continuity in the use of the *tsinza*. This will shed light on how an instrument that played a significant role in the traditional funerals has now become accepted and used at Christian funerals, thus creating one of the 'new' contexts in which the instrument is used.

8.2.4 Christian Funerals

As soon as a death is reported, people gather in the deceased's person compound, and male mourners sit separately from female mourners. Men sit in front of the deceased's compound while women sit inside. While relatives and family members weep, and mourn the deceased, friends and other village members, comprising mainly of groups in the church, engage in singing religious songs. The religious songs contain consoling words, bringing future hope to the bereaved. Two of the most prominent church groups that sing at various stages of Christian funerals are the Women Fellowship (*Zumunta Mata Ekklesiya*) and the New Life for All (*Sabon Rai Don Kowa*) singing groups. The former is a fellowship comprising of married women only, while the later is an evangelical group. The choir of both groups participates actively at the funeral of a deceased church member. The tsinza is prominent among the instruments used by both groups. Other instruments include cylindrical drums *ganga,* rattles *kace-kace,* a metal gong, and a pottery drum *humbutu.* All the instruments used by the choir groups, with the exception of the *tsinza*, are not originally Bura musical instruments.[115] They have been adopted from the Igbo culture of Southern Nigeria. The pottery drum is called *humbutu* but unlike that of the Bura, it is bigger and sphere shaped, with a small, round, open mouth. Its primary function is to produce musical bass, which is achieved by taping the open mouth with a round and flat object covered with soft textile material. The *tsinza,* though, is the lead instrument of the choir groups at most occasions.

While it is true that the use of the *tsinza* and the interpretation of the meaning of its music at Christian funerals is not seen in the same light as in the case of traditional funerals, it can be argued that such occasions have sustained the continuity of use of the instrument. Not only are new repertoires created, but also other non-Bura musical instruments accompany the *tsinza,* which is entirely different from what one would find in the traditional context. In the Christian context, it is not only Bura songs that accompany the instrument, but also church songs in other languages, particularly the Hausa language, that is widely spoken across Northern Nigeria.

Unlike in the case of traditional funerals discussed in Chapter 6 of this study, the songs that the church choirs sing accompanied by the *tsinza* at Christian funerals do not follow a specific sequence. For traditional funer-

---

115 Even the drum *Ganga* is not the Bura type.

als every step of the rites performed have specific *tsinza* music as accompaniment. This is not the case in Christian funerals, where it is left up to the discretion of the *tsinza* player to decide which songs the Christian choruses perform. The songs do not follow any specific sequence and anyone that is popular and liked by the participants can be repeated at different times throughout the course of a funeral. Even though there are no fixed tunes for specific rites in Bura Christian funerals per se, the most preferred songs by the choirs at such occasions are the ones that relate to death and life in "paradise" as reflected in teachings of the Bible. The following are some examples of such songs and their symbolic meanings:

1. Mama/Baba ga ata heni ya?
   Mother/Father are you sleeping?
2. Awa... ga ku msiri
   No...you are relieved
3. Ki akwa heaven la la
   There is a house prepared in heaven
4. Ki nga
   It is your house

The above song can be sung at either the funeral of a deceased adult Christian, regardless of gender. It implies that by dying, the deceased is going 'home' to 'paradise' where a "house" that is already prepared and awaits him or her, and would grant a 'resting place' from all the 'troubles' of the world. Such a song is not directed at a deceased person per se, but rather at the mourners. It gives assurances to the mourners of a life in "paradise" after death as contained in the teachings of the Bible. A second example of songs the choir sing at Christian funerals goes thus:

1. *Mama/Baba... mama/ baba*
   Mother/Father... mother/ father
2. *Mwari ja*
   Just go
3. *Saka an ku hara mama/baba*
   It is your time that has come
4. *Mama/Baba mwari ja*
   Mother/Father just go
5. *Sai ma yeru ku si*
   Until we arrive

Again, this song deals with the concept of 'paradise'. The song is to bid a deceased person 'farewell,' even though his or her death is considered premature. But because of the belief in the teachings of the Bible that God gives life and takes it as He pleases, the people accept it as the appropriate time for a deceased person to 'go'. Like in the first example above, this song also focuses on 'paradise' and expresses the hope of the mourners' reunification with a deceased person in 'paradise' when they die as well.

As mentioned earlier in this chapter, it is not only Bura songs that are performed with the *tsinza* at Christian funerals. Many songs are performed especially in the Hausa language. This is a complete departure from the traditional context of use of the instrument where it is believed that ancestors must be "communicated" with through the *tsinza* only in a language they "speak and understand," that being the Bura language. Generally speaking, the use of the instrument at Christian occasions has changed this belief. The change has created a "new" context of use of the *tsinza* as well. One example out of the many Hausa songs, which are performed by *tsinza* players at Christian funerals, is as follows:

1. Ka isa yabo
   You are worthy to be praised
2. Allah na sama
   God in heaven
3. Za mu yabe ka
   We will praise thee
4. Allah na sama
   God in heaven

Unlike in the examples given above, this song focuses on praising God. However, the praise is an acceptance of the Christian teaching that all things (good or bad) that happen are with the consent of God. The intention of the song is, therefore, to remind the mourners that God should be praised in all situations including the death of a loved one.

The above are a few examples of the songs that go on in the compound of the deceased as the mourners await the return of volunteers who went to the church cemetery to dig a grave. Unlike the traditional grave that is dug in the shaft and tunnel form, graves for Christian burials are dug in a rectangular form, about six feet deep and the length depending on the height of the deceased. Beer drinking and drumming does not accompany the digging, as is the case with traditional funerals.[116] Only water mixed with sorghum flour is served to the diggers. Also, as the digging goes on, back at the compound some of the deceased's relatives and volunteers bathe the body and his or her clothes are put on. If the family of the deceased can

---

116 Consumption of alchohol is not allowed in the doctrine of the E.Y.N, the dominant church in Bura land.

afford it, a coffin is provided. The corpse is put into the coffin and left open until the clergyman says the 'last' prayers.

As soon as the grave is ready, the corpse is brought out of the compound and placed where the male mourners have been sitting. If a family wishes the corpse to be taken to church for a funeral service, they will do so. Whether in a church or in front of the compound, the church choir is given the opportunity to sing again. Any of the songs performed earlier as the mourners await the completion of the digging of the grave may be repeated at this point. After the choir performs a song, the clergyman says a short sermon, dwelling mainly on the deceased's lifestyle. He goes on to urge all sympathizers at the funeral to reexamine their lifestyle to see whether they are 'living right' with God. After the short sermon by the clergy, a short prayer is said and the corpse is either carried on a bier or driven in a car to the grave. No musical instrument is taken to the graveside to direct the laying of the corpse in the grave, as is the case with traditional funerals. In the traditional context the *tsinza* is used in directing the person laying the corpse in the grave (cf. Chapter 6).

At the grave, the corpse is lowered in (if it is in a coffin) with ropes. If it is not inside a coffin, two people climb into the grave and carefully lay it on a mat. The traditional position for male and female is maintained if a coffin is not being used—a man's corpse is laid on the right side with the head to the east, facing south, with the right hand placed under the head, while a woman's is laid facing west with the left hand under the head.

Another surviving traditional practice, which I also have observed at the burials I attended, is the role of *mjir sardzi*. Depending on the relative age of a deceased, *mjir sardzi* participate actively in Christian funeral rites. If a deceased is above fifty years, they 'joke' with his or her children and relatives. However, jokes are limited to mimicking the deceased only. They do not seize the corpse and 'joke' with it, as is the case in traditional funerals. If the deceased is below the age of fifty, they do not 'joke' with his or her children during the mourning period.

After the corpse has been placed in the grave, the clergyman says another short sermon, reaffirming that man is created out of dust and unto dust he must return. As he says this, he throws some earth onto the corpse in the grave. After this, soil is shoveled into the grave (if a coffin is being used) until a mound is formed. If a coffin is not being used, a log of wood that has been cut to size is arranged over the mouth of the grave to cover it. Fresh leaves are sprinkled freely on the log of wood. Fresh mud mixed with dry grass is used to plaster over the leaves. This is to prevent soil from touching the corpse. Soil is then shoveled over it to form a mound. Stone is used to surround the mound as a demarcation. A short prayer is said again, and the mourners return to the deceased's compound to console the family once more. Close relatives of the deceased remain with the family throughout the mourning period; three days in the case of children below the age of eighteen and seven days in the case of people above eighteen years of age.

On the third or seventh day, *kilbila kusar* (a funeral service) is held. On the eve of the *kilbila kusar*, an all-night vigil is kept if the deceased is an adult. It is an occasion again where the *Zumunta Mata Ekklesia* and *Sabon Rai don Kowa* choir groups sing Christian songs led by a *tsinza* player all through the night. Most songs at an all-night vigil are repetitions of the ones sung on the first day of a burial. The songs are also not sung in a particular order and a particular song can be heard over and over again at different times of the all-night vigil.

On the morning of the *kilbila kusar* day, both men and women sit in front of the deceased's compound. The ceremony starts with a congregational hymn, one each from Bura and Hausa hymnbooks. The *Zumunta Mata Ekklesia* is also given an opportunity to sing. Again, all the singing is accompanied by the *tsinza*. Next, if the family members wish, his or her close friend reads a short biography of the deceased. The clergyman then says a short sermon and prayers. In his prayers, the clergyman specifically prays for God's guidance for the family of the deceased. Kola nuts and sweets are distributed to the people in attendance. A member of the family gives a vote of thanks and calls on anyone who owes the deceased anything to meet the family members within a period agreed upon by the family. He similarly calls on anyone who the deceased owes anything to present his or her claims. After all of this, a short prayer is said and people disperse.

The rites that follow after all the above are similar to what occurs in traditional funerals. If the deceased has children, his lineage members gather them, and they are asked to select among his brothers or relatives whom they want to be their stepfather or guardian. This person then assumes responsibility for the child. If the deceased is a woman, her children are given to her sisters or grandparents, if they are considered to be too young (i.e., up to twelve years old) to live with their father.

Christianity frowns upon widow inheritance; so the issue of inheriting a widow does not even arise. For those who defy this law, the church imposes sanctions upon them and as a result, they cannot hold any position of leadership in the church. If a widow is still young and she feels like getting married again, she goes with her family. If she decides to remain in the compound with her children, she is free to do so. However, if she chooses to remain, one of the deceased husband's lineage members is appointed to look after her needs and monitor her activities. If she is caught having love affairs with any man, she is sent packing back to her family. Her children are taken away from her as well.

As for the inheritance of a deceased's assets, it is mostly done in the traditional way at a time convenient for the deceased's children. If, however, a widow decides to stay with her children, the deceased's assets are left intact for their use. If the children of the deceased are adults, they may also decide not to divide their father's assets. They may keep them intact and use them as family property with everyone having equal access to it. In the case where a deceased left a will, it is strictly adhered to.

There is no doubt from this description of Christian funerals that the 'past' is represented in the 'present' especially in relation to the use of the *tsinza*. However, different meanings and interpretations are given to the rites performed at Christian funerals. Compared to the traditional context of the use of the *tsinza* as a medium of communication discussed in Chapter 6 of this study, the instrument appears to fulfill more of an entertainment function in its contemporary context. In Christian funerals for example, there is no emphasis on communication between the living and the dead. Rather, emphasis is placed on 'making it to paradise' as contained in Christian beliefs. There is no fear of 'offending' the *mambula* as the people have the assurances that a deceased member of their society goes to 'paradise' directly upon death. There is no fixed repertoire that the people have to adhere to in order for a *mambula* to safely be ensconced into 'paradise.' It could thus be said that the *tsinza* has lost its significance as a medium of communication in Bura Christian funerals. However, its use in Christian funerals has also definitely created a 'new' context of use, thereby, sustaining the continuity of use of the instrument by the Bura.

8.3   Conclusion

The Bura musical occasions discussed in this chapter give an insight into the significance of the *tsinza* in its contemporary context. All the musical occasions discussed in this chapter provide the 'new' contexts in which the Bura use the *tsinza*. At wedding ceremonies, the younger generations of players have found their individual styles surfacing, replacing the old ones in favor of the audience's response. Similarly, the use of the instrument in the church and at other Christian-related activities (i.e. Christian funerals) are new contexts that have created new musical orientations amongst many in Bura society. The new context of the instrument explains how the Bura have maintained the use of the *tsinza*. There appears to be the realization that the instrument can be used in many ways that do not really conflict with the teachings of the missionaries, in contrast to the view of the instrument at the beginning of the conversion of the Bura to Christianity. The adoption of Christianity is one major aspect that affected many indigenous practices of the Bura. This is especially true with regard to the *tsinza*, the principal subject of this study. The demand of the missionaries for the people to abandon their indigenous practices as a requirement for admission into the new Christian fold definitely impacted the *tsinza* tradition, as has the perception of the instrument and its music changed significantly due to this demand. The reconciliation and integration of some Bura indigenous practices with the new religious system as demonstrated, for example, in the context of use of the *tsinza* in Christian funerals, confirms the hypothesis that Christianity as a new social institution largely brought about a change in the context of use of the instrument. The perception of the instrument changed amongst many in the society. However, it was not completely abandoned, but rather a 'new' context of use emerged. The 'new' context of use can be said to have also created a new musical orientation among the people.

9   Summary and Conclusions

This thesis is about the *tsinza* xylophone, an instrument that is considered to have originally been an important funeral instrument and closely associated with Bura identity. With the beginning of missionary activities in Bura land in the early 1920s, the Bura people encountered teachings that required them to convert to a new religion, Christianity, and to denounce many of their indigenous beliefs and cultural practices. The missionaries condemned out-right what they saw of the practices of Bura traditional society and set up new requirements for entering the new Christian fold.

The *tsinza* tradition was one among many of the practices the missionaries condemned as 'evil' and, therefore, had no place in the new religion despite being an important instrument that accompanied every step of the rites performed at indigenous Bura funerals. Many of the converts abandoned the instrument at a time when they were going through a period of general confusion of dealing with the intrusion and adoption of a new religion. However, not all of the Bura people converted to Christianity. Some in the society continue to practice Bura traditional religion up to today. The instrument is, therefore, to some extent, still significant for some of the traditional practices of the non-converted Bura. For example, it remains quite an important instrument for the indigenous funerary practices of those who still practice Bura traditional religion.

Despite the initial rejection of use of the instrument by the church, it has in recent times become part of the repertoire of instruments that are used as an accompaniment to the various choir groups that sing at services both inside and outside of the church. The implication of this is that the instrument is now being used in 'new' contexts other than that which it is said to originally be used for, such as at funerals. With the conversion of many of the Bura to Christianity—and to some extent Islam, too—the perception about the *tsinza* and its music has changed. Many no longer consider the instrument as important for funerals as emphasized by the older generation. Since there is only a minority in society who still practice traditional religion, there are fewer people participating in traditional rituals. As a result of this, the traditional repertoire of funeral music is gradually disappearing. Today, however, the instrument has assumed other roles with an entirely different meaning for many in Bura society. At the core of this thesis, therefore, is an exploration of why and in what ways the Bura maintain *tsinza* music and performance even though the traditional repertoire is gradually disappearing. Specific attention is paid to the change in the context of use of the instrument. The *tsinza* is used in 'new' contexts in today's Bura society. The 'new' contexts of use appear to be one of the main reasons why *tsinza* music and performance remain a lively art amongst the Bura.

In the introduction of this thesis, I narrated my experience of the attitude demonstrated towards the instrument by my parents and adults generally in the community where I grew up. The childhood experience I related in the introductory chapter of this thesis is what triggered my interest to undertake a study of the *tsinza*. The methods used in the study and outline of the chapters also constitutes the introduction.

In Chapter 2, I explored the importance of the relationship between the past and the present in the reconstruction of music history by considering the various methods and theories put forward by ethnomusicologists who undertook research on this topic. Many of the scholars whose works I considered particularly theorized the nature of the past and present and the role of memory in reconstructing music history. Most of the theories demonstrate that the 'present' will always contain the element of the 'past,' and memories of the 'past' are constantly changing and influenced by new events that occur everyday in society. This is quite true with regard to this study and I, therefore, find the theories very relevant in my study of the *tsinza*. Some of the theories were applied to determine the elements of the 'past' that remain in the 'present'. For example, the older generation of players of the instrument is of the opinion that some of the *tsinza* music performed by the younger generation at weddings as entertainment music today, are part of the repertoire for indigenous funeral. The younger generations of players do not see it this way and have a different interpretation of their music. It is apparent that they do not cling rigidly to the old, but rather create something new out of it. This generational difference in the interpretation of the music played at weddings in present day Bura society is an indication that certain elements of the 'past' seem to be contained in the 'present.'

Wachsmann's (1971) scheme of historical investigation in ethnomusicology, in particular, has proved to be useful and it is adopted for this study. His model is one of the few theoretical models set for the study of music that considers memory in its structure. My study largely depended on the memory of my informants, as there is only very scant literature on Bura music, mostly reports by colonial officers. However, in this study, Wachsmann's scheme as applied in his own case of studying musical instruments in Kiganda tradition, is reversed. Instead of starting with the present, my investigation of the *tsinza* started with a long-distance view of the instrument reaching the present. This approach provided me with a clear picture of the change that occurred in context use of the instrument by the Bura. Thus, the 'present' use of the instrument is viewed through its 'past' use.

The regional context and environment is explored in Chapter 3. The environment of any given society plays a role in shaping and sustaining their existence. The geographical setting, the Bura worldview, the pre-colonial political structure and the colonial history of the area, are briefly discussed in this chapter to give an insight into the milieu that shaped the culture of the people. The regional context and environment constitutes a part of the 'past history' of the Bura people. I use the term 'past history' in the sense that the encounter of the Bura people with the missionaries is considered as their "immediate past history" (Bielawski 1985: 10) for the purpose of this study. The imposition of colonial rule in the area in particular could be said to mark the beginning of gradual changes—especially in terms of the political system. The colonial system did not pay any particular attention to the culture of the people by demanding that they do away with some of their practices. Rather, the interest of the system was to impose and exact control in the area by bringing it under the British Native Administration as with the other parts where the system had already been established. This, however, could be considered a factor that helped pave a way for the American missionaries to reach the area, as the missionaries were granted permission to go to the area by the colonial government.

In Chapter 4, I investigated the construction technique and history of the *tsinza*. The instrument is also considered in the context of other xylophones in Africa that have a similar order of keys. Since there is no written record on the *tsinza*, I relied more on oral information from my informants on the field to reconstruct the history of the instrument. From the accounts of my informants, three legends associated with the origin of the *tsinza* emerged. All the three legends appear to link the origin of the instrument to 'non-natural' sources. The first legend discussed in the chapter, links the origin of the instrument to a dream which led to the creation of fire with which a hoe, an important tool for the largely agrarian Bura society, was produced. The production of the hoe led to the cultivation of crops and a bumper harvest. In the process of searching for how and what to use in celebrating the bumper harvest, the *tsinza* was accidentally invented.

In the second legend, the origin of the instrument is linked to *Cicu* (one of the Bura spirit types) whom someone from the Bura Nganjiwa clan saw playing the instrument in a river. The man 'stole' the instrument and it became part and parcel of the Bura culture. The third legend linked the origin of the instrument to an earlier type that was made of cornstalk. One common feature of the legends is that in all, the origin of the instrument is portrayed as having come from a 'non-natural' source. What can, however, be deduced from the first and the third legend in particular about the origin of the instrument is that it links it to the transformation from hunting and gathering society to a cultivating one.

A case study of the construction of the *tsinza* is presented in the chapter as well. It emerged from the case study that the construction of the instrument has a special language with emphasis on *nthla kulang* (removing the "bad voice"). In the Bura worldview, the sound plates are termed as *mji* "people" with *kuraku*, "voice." For the Bura, the voices *Kuraku mji* are categorized into seven groups. A combination of the seven different *kuraku* is required for people *mji* to communicate in a 'nice' way with one another and especially with the ancestors who are considered 'non-natural' characters. As a result of this, the makers of the instrument pay a great attention to getting the 'right voice.'

In Bura taxonomy, the seven sound plates (considered to be people *mji* with different voices *kuraku*) are referred to by the following terms, beginning from the left hand side in the organology of the *tsinza*: *anggir matsikar* (the big left), *elang matsikar* (the small left), *kuba at kiri* (meet-on-me), *elang diffu* (the small middle), *anggir diffu* (the big middle), *elang mazim* (the small right) and *anggir mazim* (the big right). The sound plates are neither arranged in a rising nor falling order to achieve the right 'voice.' The instrument does not have its lowest key *elang diffu* to the extreme left; it is instead exactly in the center next to the second highest tone *anggir diffu* and the second lowest is arranged in the 2nd position to the right next to the highest tone *anggir mazim*. This arrangement gives the desired 'voice'-tone to the *tsinza*.

Two specific qualities of the instrument mark it as unique in the African context. One is the particular technique of playing this instrument: on the one hand the forked Y-shaped stick and on the other hand the order of the keys. The shape of the sticks enables the player to either beat one or two keys simultaneously. But he would only play certain plates together which, in turn, determines the uniqueness of their arrangement.

The *tsinza* is often adorned with hanging tassel carvings and other decorations. The most interesting of the decorations is the one done on the back of the *Kugwa tsinza*. The decorations on the back are formed by the use of a multiplicity of fine lines; sometimes with the interplay of figures. My investigations revealed that there are no specific rules as to which decoration should be made on a *tsinza* when it is being constructed. Sometimes the builders of the instrument make their own choices. However, the choices made by most musicians are a way of achieving recognition and prestige. Many are particular about their instrument being the best. Sometimes it is left to the discretion of the woman asked to do the decoration. However, my investigation also reveals that decorative motifs are passed from one generation to the next. There appears to be similarities in the decorative motifs of older instruments and newer ones, though styles of overall decoration do change.

In Chapter 5, I explored the relationship between language and musical instruments. Apart from the *tsinza*, the Bura people have other musical instruments. The chapter focused mainly on the description of other musical instruments of the people, words or terminology describing them and their different ways of being played. The terminology used by a culture primarily reflects that culture's interest and concerns. My investigation of the relationship between language and musical instruments in this chapter is based on Sapir's (1964) theory, which proposes that, "language helps define the worldview of its speakers". It does so, according to him, "in part, by providing labels for certain kinds of phenomena (things, concepts, qualities, and actions), which different languages define according to different criteria" (Peoples and Alan 1991: 62). Bura terms used in describing musical instruments, and the ways they are played, are explored in the chapter to determine whether some aspects of the people's worldview are embedded in the language used in discussing musical performances generally.

It does emerge from my investigation that some Bura words or terms that relate to music making are also used in everyday language to describe different things, actions and concepts that reflect some of the belief and value system of the society. In the language used in the construction of the *tsinza*, for example, the instrument is given human attributes. The sound plates are referred to as *mji* people having different *kuraku* voice. The variety in the *kuraku* is important in talking nicely with one another. This is similar to the other Bura instruments, where certain actions that are only carried out by humans can be employed in describing actions associated with musical performances. For example, a drum that is beaten loud is described as *Ganga ni a tuwa*. A direct English translation of this would mean, "the drum is crying". "Crying" is mainly associated with human beings but in the case of the Bura, it is also used in describing a drum that is beaten loudly. Thus, the relationship between language and musical instruments is important in understanding certain aspects of the Bura worldview.

Chapter 6 investigated the *tsinza* in its traditional context. The instrument is considered originally to have been an important funeral instrument. Its use at Bura funerals is explored to determine the role it plays during such occasions. The chapter reviewed some of the literature that relates to death-related behavior, which is of crucial importance to many of the central theoretical developments in anthropology since its beginnings. The review is done with the view of understanding Bura death-related behavior by placing such in the context of the theories reviewed. Funerals within Northeast Nigeria are found to be one rite within an interrelated ritual complex pertaining to several domains: death itself, inheritance, ancestralization, and the relationship between the dead and the living.

To understand the several rites performed within each of the domains to safely ensconce the spirit of the dead to the ancestral world, a reconstruction of Bura funerals for the various categories of its members (i.e. adult male, adult female, young person, a chief, and someone killed by lightening) is undertaken in Chapter 6. The reconstruction is necessary in order to understand the significance of the *tsinza* in Bura funeral and to determine the repertoire as well. However, the reconstruction is undertaken although I am conscious of the fact that there is no 'standard funeral' in any given society. The data presented is, therefore, based on the memory of my informants of the rites that are performed at Bura funerals. I had the opportunity of participating and observing an indigenous Bura funeral during the course of the fieldwork for this study, which allowed me to directly observe the use of the *tsinza* in a funerary context. It also provided the opportunity of noting the rites accompanied by *tsinza* music. This was important because the scant literature on Bura funerals mentions music being played at certain stages of a funeral, without making clear what type of music and what purpose it serves.

Each step of the rites of the funeral I observed and presented as a case study in Chapter 6 was accompanied by *tsinza* music. My understanding of the significance of the instrument in funerals led me to propose a theory that the instrument is used as a means of 'mediation' between the living and the dead in the efforts of the former to safely ensconce the *mambula* (soul) of the deceased into the ancestral world. In the people's worldview, the *mambula* of a deceased member of their family does not depart to the ancestral world immediately. It hovers about in the trees of the compound to see whether the appropriate rites are performed or not. The *mambula*, which is in a liminal state, is considered to be 'dangerous' and can cause misfortune or sicknesses to the living members of his or her family if the appropriate rites are not performed. In the Bura worldview, communicating with the *mambula*, which is considered 'invincible' is only possible through the 'mediation' of the *tsinza* and its music. Generally speaking, the Bura believe that it is impossible to communicate with 'non-natural forces.' They believe in the existence of such 'forces' and also believe in the inability to reach them directly. For example, the people believe in the existence of the *hyel* god that cannot be reached directly but only through a smaller god *haptu*. *Haptu*, therefore, serves as a 'mediator' between the people and *hyel*.

The *tsinza* seems to fulfill a similar role at Bura indigenous funerals. It is at the center of the communication between the living body and *mambula* of a deceased that has become 'invincible' and, therefore, directly unreachable. The story of Bura origin of death itself is used to illustrate the people's reliance on a 'mediator' to 'communicate' with 'non-natural forces.' In the story a worm *Kulamya* served as the 'mediator' between the people and *Hyel* when a member of their society died and they did not know what to do with the body; the living members of the deceased's society did not ask *Hyel* directly what to do. In a similar manner, in carrying out the appropriate rites that the people came up with to dispose a deceased member of their society after not doing what *hyel* asked them to do, the living do not 'communicate' with the body and *mambula* that has become 'invincible' directly. Rather, the *tsinza* is at the center as a 'mediator' between the living, the body and *mambula* in the living's effort to safely ensconce the deceased in the ancestral world. Thus, in its traditional context, the *tsinza* is a medium through which 'communication' between the living and the dead is facilitated in an attempt to safely establish the *mambula* of a deceased into the ancestral world.

In Chapter 7, I turned to what can be termed as the "immediate past history" (Bielawski 1985: 10) of the people, in this case, the encounter with the missionary work that started in the area in 1922. The chapters that preceded Chapter 7 could be referred to as the 'past history' of the Bura people in that it focused on the oral history of what the pre-missionaries practices were and how they are carried out still today . For the 'immediate past history' of the people, I, therefore, explored the history of the arrival of the missionaries and the impact it had on their traditional practices. The commencement of missionary work in Bura land was one major event that caused a significant shift in the history of the people. Ever since the people came into contact with the missionaries from the Church of the Brethren in America (CBM), many of their traditional practices were either completely abandoned or underwent significant changes. This happened largely due to the fact that the missionaries considered many of the indigenous practices of the people as 'evil' and, therefore, not acceptable in meeting the requirements set for entering the 'new' religion. The educational and health care system introduced by the missionaries also offered a new way of life for the people. Many were attracted to the new religion because of this new way of life. As a result, the converts abandoned many of their indigenous cultural practices in order to fit into the new Christian community. One of the greatest impacts of the missionaries was, therefore, the replacement of the Bura traditional religion with the new Christian faith. Since the Bura culture was basically a religious culture and its customs and behavior were so closely tied to religious beliefs, the missionaries, in attempting to convert the people to a new way of life struck at the core of the old patterns.

The basis for conversion to the new faith emphasized the "exalted individual" (Ayandele, 1966:330). For the missionary, the individual must build and maintain his or her own personal faith and relationship with God. The individual and not the family, group, clan or tribe must make the decision.[117] Consequently, individuals, not social units, were converted. This cultural confrontation was a direct disruption of the indigenous communal Bura tribal solidarity. As observed by one of the pioneer missionaries in Bura land, H.S. Kulp:

> The Bura lives in collectivistic stage, that is to say there is no recognition of individuality. All through life remains a unit in a group, and he thinks himself as such, he is a member of his age grade, and of his tribe (Kulp, 1924-26: 4).

---

117 Bura people traditionally viewed themselves as Banu, Malgwi, Mshelia, Bwala, Tarfa and so on. In other words, clans and sub-clans were originally primary identity groups within Bura locale.

From Kulp's statement, it is clear that before many got converted to Christianity the Bura acted as a group. By implication this means that participation in rituals involved all in the society. Perhaps then, the disruption caused by conversion to Christianity is better seen in the light of the people abandoning many rituals that were key in forging solidarity in the society. One such key ritual abandoned among many by the converts was the indigenous funeral rite where the *tsinza* played a significant role.

With the introduction of Christianity, music that hitherto played a central role in all Bura rituals became restricted. Converts were not permitted to dance to any form of music, even at Christian occasions. Dancing to traditional music, therefore, seemed even more 'evil' since it was often a part of rituals and ceremonies, which involved supplications to the spirits (*shatan*). This had a significant impact on the *tsinza* and its music, which prior to the conversion of many to Christianity, have been said to be an important funeral instrument.

My investigation, however, revealed that there is no existing written law anywhere in the documents of the church that prevents the people from using traditional musical instruments in church services on Sundays or any other Christian occasions. The non-acceptance of the use of the instrument in the church was rather a policy that existed because of the teaching of the missionaries on some of the cultural practices of the people as being 'evil.' The *tsinza*, therefore, gradually found its way into the church after the missionaries handed control to the people, and in particular, when they realized that they do not have to be stripped of their culture completely to live within the culture of the missionaries and vice versa. Today, the instrument is used in the church and all other Christian occasions that require music. Though, the meaning of the music and its function is completely understood in a different way from the traditional context by the generation of the educated Bura elites that emerged as a result of the missionaries' endeavors in the field of education. Many of the elites abandoned some of the practices and belief systems that they consider not to conform to the 'learned' Western way of thinking. The *tsinza* and the meaning of its music are, therefore, understood in a different way in contemporary Bura society. This perhaps plays a roll in the 'new' context of use of the instrument that has emerged in 'modern' Bura society.

In Chapter 8, I explored the *tsinza* in its contemporary context. There is no doubt that the "immediate past history" (Bielawski 1985: 10) of the Bura (the encounter with Christianity), changed the perception of the people with regard to the *tsinza*. The perception of the instrument as being a funeral instrument has changed gradually. Although the instrument is still regarded by the unconverted Bura as very important for indigenous funeral rites, it is also used in other contexts in contemporary Bura society. Today, it is used not only as part of Bura ensembles that perform dance music *bansuwe* for entertainment and to celebrate traditional festivities that have also taken new forms, but it is also used in Christian and Muslim festivities that require music. The instrument is also played solo or accompanied by rattle players to entertain guests at *kildzi/lausa* weddings. These are all 'new' contexts in which the instrument is used.

The use of the instrument at *kildzi/lausa,* in particular, seems to have created generational differences in the understanding of the instrument and its music. The older generation of players is of the opinion that the music performed by the younger generation, who perform mainly at weddings, contains funeral music. In contrast, the younger generation say that their patrons from whom they receive monetary rewards for singing their 'praise', simply want to dance. They, therefore, play any tune considered to be danceable, not minding whether it is funeral music or not. They appear not to cling rigidly to the old pattern of the music, but create something 'new' out of it.

Perhaps, one of the 'new' contexts that is more interesting is the instrument's use in Christian funerals as also explored in Chapter 8. To understand how the Bura maintain the use of the *tsinza* is perhaps through its use at Christian funerals. There is no doubt that the description of Christian funeral rites provided in Chapter 8 clearly shows a kind of reconciliation and integration of Bura indigenous practices with a new religious system. The *tsinza* continued to be used at funerals after it found its way into the church, but its use at Christian funerals carries a different meaning for the adherents of the religion. At Christian funerals, for example, the instrument is no longer considered as a medium of 'communication' as I theorized for its use in the traditional context, but rather serves more of an entertainment and an avenue of assuring the adherents of the Christian faith through its music of a life in paradise after death. In the Christian context, therefore, the Christianized Bura no longer recognize the significance of the instrument as a 'mediator' between the living and a *mambula* that need to be safely ensconced in the ancestral world. The songs are directed more towards the living members of the Christian fold. This is remarkably different from the traditional context where the concern is more on the dead whose *mambula* needs 'communicating' with through the *tsinza* in order to be separated from the living and established in the ancestral world.

The 'new' contexts of use of the instrument no doubt provide continuity for the *tsinza*. However, going by Bates' (2012) theory that the study of musical instruments should go beyond just the study of organology but that of the social life as well, the *tsinza* should be seen as more than just an instrument. The instrument can be seen in the light of Bates' theory to have its own social life. It is true that its construction technique and organology remain the same and its context of uses have changed, but it can also be said that the instrument has changed the contexts within which the people use it as well. It is not just an instrument that is associated with Bura rituals but one that, in contemporary times, the people use for fostering social solidarity as well. Thus, the Bura have perhaps maintained the use of the instrument, which having been said to be closely linked with their identity, because in the present-day context of Nigeria, it might be more important to stress their cultural affiliation as an ethnic group through xylophone music rather than specific clan or religious affiliations within their contemporary social order. The Christianization of the majority of the Bura no doubt affected the traditional social systems, but to identify as a group of people in present day Nigeria, *tsinza* music seems to be a rallying point. However, the instrument should not only be seen as "central to Bura social networks, but also itself as an actor with agency" (Bates, 2012: 364). It has lived through the culture of the people since times immemorial and has perhaps at different times created 'new culture' amongst the Bura people. 'New culture' in the sense that the instrument has not only remained in the domain of funeral rituals, in which it has been said to play an important role, but has moved to other domains as well in contemporary Bura society. Its move to other domains by the people created a change, but it has also maintained continuity as well. The instrument, therefore, is an actor with agency that plays a significant role in shaping some aspects of Bura culture.

Bibliography

Adeleye, R. A. 1971. Power and diplomacy in Northern Nigeria, 1804-1906; the Sokoto Caliphate and its enemies. New York: Humanities Press.

Agawu, V Kofi. 1988. "Music in the funeral traditions of the Akpafu." Ethnomusicology: 75-105.

Ajayi, J. F. Ade Crowder Michael. 1972. History of West Africa. New York: Columbia University Press.

Ajuwon, Bade. 1982. Funeral dirges of Yoruba hunters. New York: NOK Publishers International.

Akyeampong, Emmanuel Kwaku, Bates Robert H. Nunn Nathan Robinson James A. 2014. Africa's development in historical perspective.

Anderson, L. 1967. The African Xylophone. African Arts. Vol. 1. Issue 1.: 46

Aning, B. A. 1967. An annotated bibliography of music and dance in English-speaking Africa. Legon: Institute of African Studies, University of Ghana.

———. 1968. "Wangara xylophone and its music." Papers in African studies. no. 3: 57-63.

———. 1968. "Factors That Shape and Maintain Folk Music in Ghana." Journal of the International Folk Music Council no. 20: 13-17.

———. 1972. "The music and musical instruments of West Africa." Brief sketches in Akan (Ghana) art symbols: literature, music and African theatre.:9-14.

———. 1976. "An historical survey of music in Ghana (with instruments)." Ghana talks.:229-241.

———. 1989. "Lakraba Lobi: master xylophonist of Ghana." African musicology: current trends: a festschrift presented to J.H. Kwabena Nketia / Jacqueline Cogdell DjeDje, editor and William G. Carter, associate editor.:93-110.

Aubert, Laurent. 2001. Cahiers de musiques traditionnelles. XIV (2001): Le geste musical. Vol. 14. Genève: Genève: Georg.

Ayandele, Emmanuel Ayankanmi. 1966. The missionary impact on modern Nigeria, 1842-1914: a political and social analysis. London: Longmans.

Bae, Yoo Jin, Avorgbedor Daniel Kodzo, Powell Susan. 2001. The distribution, construction, tuning, and performance technique of the African log xylophone. Ohio State University School of Music.

Baldwin, Alma Ferne. 1973. "The impact of American missionaries on the Bura people of Nigeria."

Barra Rodríguez, Manuel. 1982. "La música entre los Jerónimos de Bornos (Cádiz)." Revista de musicología no. 5 (2):235-286.

———. 1983. "El órgano de la parroquia de Bornos (Cádiz)." Collected Work: Homenaje a Samuel Rubio. (AN: 1983-07945). no. 6 (1-2):149-164.

Barz, Gregory F. Cooley Timothy J. 2008. Shadows in the field new perspectives for fieldwork in ethnomusicology. Oxford University Press.

Bates, Eliot. 2012. "The social life of musical instruments." Ethnomusicology 56(3): 363-395.

Berlin, Gabriele, and Artur Simon. 2002. Music archiving in the world. Berlin: Berlin: VWB: Verlag für Wissenschaft und Bildung.

Berliner, Paul. 1978. The soul of mbira : music and traditions of the Shona people of Zimbabwe. Berkeley: University of California Press.

Berns, Marla. 1985. "Decorated gourds of Northeastern Nigeria." African arts. no. 19:28-45.

Bielawski, Ludwik Wiewiorkowski Ludwik. 1985. "History in Ethnomusicology." Yearbook for Traditional Music 17: 8-15.

Bithell, Caroline. 2006. The past in music. Abingdon: Routledge.

Bittinger, Desmond W. 1938. The Soudan's second sunup. Elgin, Ill.: Elgin Press.

———. 1939. Land of the monkey bread tree. Elgin, Ill.: General Mission Board, Church of the Brethren.

———. 1941. An educational experiment in northern Nigeria in its cultural setting, Philadelphia.

———. 1952. The Church of the Brethren. Elgin, IL: General Brotherhood Board, Church of the Brethren.

———. 1978. The song of the drums : African life and love under the monkey bread tree. New York: Vantage Press.

Blacking, John. 1977. "Some Problems of Theory and Method in the Study of Musical Change." Yearbook of the International Folk Music Council. 9:1-26.

Blench, Roger. 1999. Bura Dictionary.

———. 2009. Bura Phonology and some suggestions concerning the orthography.

Bohlman, Philip V. 2008. "Returning to the Ethnomusicological Past." Shadows in the Field: New Perspective for Fieldwork in Ethnomusicology. 2nd Edition Barz Cooley & Timothy J. Oxford University Press, New York.

Boone, Olga. 1936. Les xylophones du Congo belge. Tervueren, Belgique: Musèe du Congo belge.

Bradbury, R. E. 1965. "Father and senior son in Edu mortuary ritual." African systems of thought:96-121.

Branger, Daniële. 1993. "Le xylophone ‡ rèsonateurs multiples des lobi." Images d'Afrique et sciences sociales: les pays lobi, birifor et dagara (Burkina Faso, CÙte d'Ivoire et Ghana): actes du colloque de Ouagadougou, 10-15 dÈcembre 1990.:460-469.

Brow, James. 1990. "Notes on community, hegemony, and the uses of the past." Anthropological quarterly 63 (1): 1-6.

Cannell, Fenella. 2006. The anthropology of Christianity. Durham: Duke University Press.

Chiener, Chou. 2002. "Experience and fieldwork: a native researcher's view." Ethnomusicology 46 (3): 456-486.

Church of the, Brethren. 1958. Kakadu ar ha ka sur vunkir sili aka hyel: songs and psalms of praise in Bura. Northern Nigeria; Lagos [Nigeria]: Church of the Brethren Mission; Printed at the Niger-Challenge Press.

Cohen, Ronald. 1974. "The evolution of hierarchical institutions: a case study from Biu, Nigeria." Savanna: a journal of the environmental and social sciences Savanna no. 3 (2):153-174.

———. 1983. "Dynastic tradition and the state." annals of Borno no. 1 (1):45-55.

Cohen, Ronald Middleton John. 1977. Comparative political systems: studies in the politics of pre-industrial societies. Austin: University of Texas Press.

Cohen, Ronald Toland Judith D. 1988. State formation and political legitimacy. New Brunswick, U.S.A.: Transaction Books.

Crampton, E. P. T. 1975. Christianity in northern Nigeria. [Place of publication not identified]: [publisher not identified].

Crozier, D. H. Blench R. Hansford Keir Nigerian Educational Research, Language Development Centre University of Ilorin Department of Linguistics Development Council, and Summer Institute of Linguistics Nigerian Languages. 1992. An index of Nigerian languages. Dallas, Tex.: Summer Institute of Linguistics.

Daniel, A. 2001. The Distribution, Construction, Tuning, and Performance Technique of the African Log Xylophone, The Ohio State University.

Davies, J. G. Northern Region of Nigeria Literature Agency. 1954. The Biu book; a collation and reference book on Biu Division (Northern Nigeria). Zaria: NORLA.

Deliège, Irène, and Ian Cross. 1993. Music and the cognitive sciences 1990: Proceedings of Cambridge Conference on Music and the Cognitive Sciences, 1990. Vol. 9, Physical Medium: Conference Source: 2nd International Conference on Music and the Cognitive Sciences : Cambridge. Yverdon: Yverdon: Harwood Academic.

Dietz, Betty Warner Olatunji Babatunde. 1965. Musical instruments of Africa; their nature, use, and place in the life of a deeply musical people. New York: John Day Co.

Dunch, Ryan. 2002. "Beyond Cultural Imperialism: Cultural Theory, Christian Missions, and Global Modernity." HITH History and Theory no. 41 (3):301-325.

Faw, Chalmer Ernest. 1973. Lardin Gabas: a land, a people, a church. Elgin, IL: Brethren Press.

Fiawoo, D. K. 1968. "From cult to "church": a study of some aspects of religious change in Ghana." Ghana journal of sociology Ghana Journal of Sociology no. 4 (2):72-87.

Fortes, Meyer. 1959. Oedipus and Job in West African religion. Cambridge [Eng.: University Press.

———. 1972. "Some reflections on ancestor worship in Africa." African systems of thought: studies presented and discussed at the third International African Seminar.

Frobenius, Leo. 1899. The origin of African civilizations. Washington.

Gabel, Creighton Bennett Norman R. Northwestern University. 1967. Reconstructing African culture history. Boston: Boston University Press.

Gaiya, Musa A. B. 2004. "Christianity in Northern Nigeria, 1975-2000." Exchange: bulletin de littÈrature des Èglises du Tiers Monde Exchange no. 33 (4):354-371.

Ga'anda District Miscellaneous Papers 1928-1939, Yola Prof. G. 2. S. N. N. A. K. (author unknown)

Garcia, Maria Elena. 2000. "Ethnographic responsibility and the anthropological endeavor: beyond identity discourse." Anthropological quarterly.

Geertz, Clifford. 1974. ""From the native's point of view" : on the nature of anthropological understanding." Meaning in anthropology Symbolic anthropology: a reader in the study of symbols and meanings Culture theory: essays on mind, self, and emotion.

———. 1983. Local knowledge: further essays in interpretive anthropology. New York: Basic Books.

Gellner, Ernest. 1987. Culture, identity, and politics. Cambridge; New York: Cambridge University Press.

Gennep, Arnold van. 1960. The rites of passage. Chicago: University of Chicago Press.

Geschiere, Peter. 2005. "Funerals and belonging: different patterns in south Cameroon." African studies review 48: 45-64.

Gilliland, Dean S. 1986. African religion meets Islam: religious change in northern Nigeria. Lanham, MD: University Press of America.

Godsey, Larry Dennis. 1980. The use of the xylophone in the funeral ceremony of the Birifor of Northwest Ghana.

Goodenough, Ward Hunt. 1970. Description and comparison in cultural anthropology. Chicago: Aldine Pub. Co.

Goody, Jack. 1975. "Religion, social change and the sociology of conversion." Changing social structure in Ghana; essays in the comparative sociology of a new state and an old tradition / ed. with an introd. by J. Goody: 91-106.

Gregory, Kathleen L. 1983. "Native-View Paradigms: Multiple Cultures and Culture Conflicts in Organizations." Administrative Science Quarterly no. 28 (3): 359-76.

Grimes, Ronald L. 1982. Beginnings in ritual studies. Washington, D.C.: University Press of America.

Hampton, Barbara L. 1982. Music and ritual symbolism in the Ga funeral.

Harold, Scheub. 2000. "Hyel and the Corpse in the Tree (Bura, Pabir/ Nigeria)."

Hartmann, K, Malte Zimmerman. 2012. Focus Marking in Bura: semantic uniformity matches syntactic heterogeneity. Natural Sciences and Linguistic Theory 30/4: 1061-1108.

Haruna, Zainab K. 1998. Bura folksongs: an analysis of their types, occasions, themes, techniques and functions, Memorial University of Newfoundland.

Headland, Thomas N., Pike Kenneth L., Harris Marvin. 1990. Emics and etics: the insider/outsider debate, Newbury Park, CA: American Anthropological Association Annual Meeting.

Helser, Albert D. 1926. In sunny Nigeria; experiences among a primitive people in the interior of North Central Africa. New York: Fleming H. Revell.

———. 1930. African stories. New York: Fleming H. Revell.

Helser, Albert D. Carney Mabel. 1934. Education of primitive people. New York [usw.]: Revell.

Heussler, Robert. 1968. The British in Northern Nigeria. London; New York: Oxford U.P.

Hewby, W.P. (1937) Accounts of Administrative History of the Gujba Pagan and Biu Division, Biu Dist. 417, N. N. A. K.

Hill, Barbara Ann Deakin University Faculty of Arts Deakin University School of History Heritage, and Society. 2004. The identity and autonomy of the indigenous community within Christianity.

Hiskett, M. 1967. "S. J. Hogben and A. H. M. Kirkgreene: The emirates of Northern Nigeria: a preliminary survey of their historical traditions. London: Oxford University Press, 1966. 70s." Bulletin of the School of Oriental and African Studies Bulletin of the School of Oriental and African Studies no. 30 (01).

Hoffmann, Carl. 1963. A grammar of the Margi language. London: Published for the International African Institute by the Oxford University Press.

Hona District Miscellaneous Papers, Yola Prof. G. 2. R. N. N. A. K. (author and date of publication unknown).

Hood, Mantle. 1982. The ethnomusicologist. Kent, Ohio: Kent State University Press.

Hornbostel, Erich Moritz von. 1933. The ethnology of African sound instruments. [S.l.]: International Institute of African Languages and Cultures.

———. 1933. "The ethnology of African sound instruments (continued)." Africa : journal of the International African Institute = revue de l'Institut africain international.

Huntington, R and Peter Metcalf. 1991. *Celebrations of Death: The anthropology of of mortuary ritual*. Cambridge University Press. Cambridge.

Inter-synodical Evangelical Lutheran Orient Mission Society, Wee M. O. Lutheran Orient Mission Society. 1921. *Report from Mission Conference held at Grace Lutheran Church, Columbus, Ohio, April 14th to 19th, 1921.* St. Paul, Minn.: Lutheran Orient Mission Society.

International Communication, Association. *Communication theory.* Oxford University Press on behalf of the International Communication Association 1991.

Jindra, Michael. 1997. *The proliferation of ancestors: death celebrations in the Cameroon Grassfields.*

Jindra, Michael, and Noret Joîl. 2011. *Funerals in Africa: explorations of a social phenomenon*. New York: Berghahn Books.

Johnston, Thomas F. 1976. "How to Make a Tsonga Xylophone." *Music Educators Journal* no. 63 (3):38-49.

Jones, A. M. 1971. *Africa and Indonesia; the evidence of the xylophone and other musical and cultural factors*. Leiden: E.J. Brill.

Kaemmer, John E. 1989. *Social power and musical change among the Shona.*

Kerschbaumer, Franz, Thomas Phleps, Bernd Hoffmann, and Franz Krieger. 2002. *Festschrift Ekkehard Jost zum 65. Geburtstag*. Vol. 34.

Kirby, Percival Robson. 1965. *The musical instruments of the native races of South Africa*. Johannesburg: Witwatersrand University Press.

Kirby, P. R. 1968. "Two curious resonated xylophones from Nigeria." *African Studies African Studies* 27 (3):141-144.

Kirk-Greene, A. H. M. 1965. *The principles of native administration in Nigeria; selected documents, 1900-1947*. London: Oxford University Press.

Knight, Roderic C. 1974. "Record reviews." *Ethnomusicology: Journal of the Society for Ethnomusicology* 18 (2):337-39.

Komolafe, Sunday Jide. 2013. *The transformation of African Christianity : development and change in the Nigerian church*. Carlisle: Langham Monographs.

Kubik, Gerhard. 1964. "Xylophone Playing in Southern Uganda." *The Journal of the Royal Anthropological Institute of Great Britain and Ireland* no. 94 (2): 138-159.

Kulp, Mary Ann Moyer. 1968. *No longer strangers; a biography of H. Stover Kulp*. Elgin, Ill.: Brethren Press.

Maddieson, Ian. 1983. "The analysis of complex phonetic elements in Bura and the syllable." *Studies in African linguistics* no. 14 (3): 285-310.

Magowan, Fiona. 2007. *Melodies of mourning : music & emotion in Northern Australia*. Oxford; Santa Fe, N.M.; Crawley, W.A.: James Currey; School for Advanced Research Press ; University of Western Australia.

Malinowski, Bronislaw. 1954. *Magic, science and religion : and other essays*. Garden City, N.Y.: Doubleday.

Maxwell, Heather A. 1999. "West Africa: when the xylophone speaks." *Turn up the volume!: a celebration of African music.*:58-67.

Meek, C. K. 1931. *Tribal studies in northern Nigeria.* London: K. Paul, Trench, Trubner & Co., ltd.

Mensah, Atta Annan. 1967. "Further notes in Ghana's xylophone traditions." *Research review* 3: 62-65.

———. 1967. "The Polyphony of Gyil-gu, Kudzo and Awutu Sakumo." *Journal of the International Folk Music Council* 19: 75-79.

———. 1982. "Gyil: the Dagara-Lobi xylophone." *Journal of African studies* 9: 139-154.

Merriam, Alan P. 1964. *The anthropology of music.* [Evanston, Ill.: Northwestern University Press.

———. 1982. "The use of music as a technique of reconstructing culture history in Africa." *African music in perspective.*: 295-320.

———. 1982. *African music in perspective.* New York: Garland.

Metcalf, Peter Huntington Richard. 1991. *Celebrations of death : the anthropology of mortuary ritual.* Cambridge: Cambridge University Press.

Mshelia, J. A. 1988. "A History of Garkida 1923 - 1973. M.A. Dissertation, Department of History, University of Maiduguri.

Montandon, George. 1919. *La gÈnÈalogie des instruments de musique et les cycles de civilisation: Ètude suivie du catalogue des instruments de musique du MusÈe ethnographique de GenÈve.* GenÈve: A. Kundig.

Moyer, Elgin Sylvester. 1931. Missions in the Church of the Brethren; their development and effect upon the denomination, Brethren Pub. House, Elgin, Ill.

Mtaku, Christopher, and Artur Simon. 1994. „Avi Pwasi, eine Musikerpersönlichkeit aus Borno: In Interview und Selbstdarstellung." Collected Work: For Gerhard Kubik: Festschrift on the occasion of his 60th birthday. Pages: 83-145. (AN: 1995-05383).

Mtaku, Christopher Y. 2005. Bura xylophone tradition. Paper read at Man and the lake: proceedings of the 12th Mega Chad Conference: Maiduguri, 2nd-9th December 2003.

Mu'azu, Mohammed Aminu, and Balami Fibi. 2010. A descriptive analysis of Bura verbs and vocabulary. M‚nchen: Lincom Europa.

Nettl, Bruno. 1964. Theory and method in ethnomusicology. [New York: Free Press of Glencoe.

Nettl, Bruno, and Stone Ruth M. Porter James Rice Timothy. 1998. The Garland encyclopedia of world music. New York: Garland Pub.

Nettl, Bruno, and Stone Ruth M. Porter James Rice Timothy Alexander Street Press. The Garland encyclopedia of world music online. Alexander Street Press 2006. Available from http://glnd.alexanderstreet.com.

Nketia, J. H. Kwabena. 1963. *African music in Ghana.* [Evanston, Ill.]: Northwestern University Press.

―――. 1966. *Music in African cultures: a review of the meaning and signif-icance of traditional African music.* [Legon]: Institute of African Studies, University of Ghana.

―――. 1969. *Funeral dirges of the Akan people.* New York: Negro Universities Press.

―――. 1974. *The music of Africa.* New York: W.W. Norton.

Nketia, J. H. Kwabena DjeDje Jacqueline Cogdell. 1984. *Studies in African music.* Los Angeles: Program in Ethnomusicology, Dept. of Music, University of California, Los Angeles.

Peoples, James G. Bailey Garrick Alan. 1991. *Humanit : an introduction to cultural anthropology.* St. Paul: West Pub. Co.

Perham, Margery Freda. 1937. *Native administration in Nigeria.* London; New York [etc.: Oxford University Press.

Preciado, Dionisio. 1983. *Homenaje a Samuel Rubio.* Vol. 6.

Quarterly and Annual reports on Biu Division 1924, Biu Dist. H.9, N. N. A. K. (author unknown).

Robson, Laura. *Colonialism and Christianity in Mandate Palestine.* University of Texas Press 2011. Available from http://search.ebscohost.com/login.aspx?direct=true&scope=site&db=nlebk&db=nlabk&AN=405323.

Ronk, Albert T. 1971. *History of Brethren missionary movements.* Ashland, Ohio: Printed by Brethren Pub. Co.

Rumsey, Alan. 2004. "Christianity, Culture Change, and the Anthropology of Ethics." *Anthropological quarterly* 77(3):581-593.

Sachs, C. 1965. *The history of musical instruments.* London.

Saighoe, Francis A. Kobina. 1991. *The music behavior of Dagaba immigrants in Tarkwa, Ghana: a study of situational change.*

Sapir, Edward. 1988. "The status of linguistics as a science." *High points in anthropology:*143-148.

Schmidhofer, August, Dietrich Schüller, and David K. Rycroft. 1994. *For Gerhard Kubik: Festschrift on the occasion of his 60th birthday, Vergleichende Musikwissenschaft.* Frankfurt am Main: Frankfurt am Main: Peter Lang.

Seavoy, Mary H. 1984. *The Sisaala xylophone tradition.* Ann Arbor, Mich.: Univ. Microfilms.

Shelemay, Kay Kaufman. 2006. "Music, Memory and History." Ethnomusi-cology Forum 15 (1): 17-37.

Sheriff, Bosoma, Mai Mallam Kuwuma, and Raimund Vogels. 2002.Simon, Artur. 2002. "Recordings of the music in Borno, north-eastern state of Nigeria, Africa." *Collected Work: Festschrift Ekkehard Jost zum 65. Ge-burtstag.* (AN: 2002-04044). 34: 215-230.

―――. 2004. "Xylophone musics in Nigeria and Cameroon." *Collected Work: 37th world conference of the International Council for Traditional Music: Conference contributions—Abstracts. Pages: 190-192. (AN: 2004-02020).*

Simon, Artur, and György Ligeti. 2000. *Das Berliner Phonogramm-Archiv 1900-2000: Sammlungen der traditionellen Musik der Welt/The Berlin Phonogramm-Archiv, 1900-2000: Collections of traditional music of the world*. Berlin: Berlin: VWB: Verlag für Wissenschaft und Bildung.

Stokes, Martin. 1994. *Ethnicity, identity, and music: the musical construction of place*. Oxford, UK; Providence, RI: Berg.

Stroux, P. Christoph. 1987. "Marimba instromento de gentili Africani." *SAMUS: South African journal of musicology/Suid-Afrikaanse tydskrif vir musiekwetenskap* no. 7:89-90.

Strumpf, Mitchel. 1970. *Ghanaian xylophone studies*. Legon: Institute of African Studies, University of Ghana.

Strumpf, Mitchel University of Ghana Institute of African Studies. 1970. *Ghanaian xylophone studies*. Legon: Institute of African Studies, University of Ghana.

Temple, O. Temple C. L. 1967. *Notes on the tribes, provinces, emirates, and states of the northern provinces of Nigeria*. New York: Barnes & Noble.

Thomas, Nicholas. 1989. *Out of time: history and evolution in anthropological discourse*. Cambridge [England]; New York: Cambridge University Press.

Thomasson, Kermon. 1973. *The missionaries and the major*.

Turner, Victor W. 1969. *The ritual process: structure and anti-structure*. Chicago: Aldine Pub. Co.

———. 1986. *The anthropology of performance*. New York: PAJ Publications.

Udo, Reuben K. 1970. *Geographical regions of Nigeria*. Berkeley: University of California Press.

Unsettled Areas, 1917-1932, Biu Dist. 259, N. N. A. K. (Author and date of publication unknown

Usman, Yusufu Bala Alkali Nur. 1983. *Studies in the history of pre-colonial Borno*. Zaria: Northern Nigerian.

Gennep, Arnold van. 1960. *The rites of passage*. Chicago: University of Chicago Press.

Vercelli, Michael Biagio. *Performance Practice of the Dagara-Birifor Gyil Tradition Through the Analysis of the Bewaa and Daarkpen Repertoire*. University of Arizona 2006. Available from http://etd.library.arizona.edu/etd/GetFileServlet?file=file:///data1/pdf/etd/azu_etd_1895_1_m.pdf&type=application/pdf.

Vereker, S.H.P. 1947. *Hona-Bura Sub-district assessment report, July 1914*. Yola Prof. G.2. U, N. N. A. K.

Vogels, Raimund, and Caroline Diessel. 2000. "Das Borno Music Documentation Project (B.M.D.P.) in Nigeria/B.M.D.P.: The Borno Music Documentation Project in Nigeria." *Collected Work: Das Berliner Phonogramm-Archiv 1900-2000: Sammlungen der traditionellen Musik der Welt/The Berlin Phonogramm-Archiv, 1900-2000: Collections of traditional music of the world*. Pages: 178-185. (AN: 2000-38468).

Von Hornbostel, E. M. 1933. "The Ethnology of African Sound-Instruments. Comments on „Geist und Werden der Musikinstrumente" by C. Sachs." *Africa: Journal of the International African Institute* 6 (2):129-157.

Wachsmann, Klaus. 1958. "A Century of Change in the Folk Music of an African Tribe." *Journal of the International Folk Music Council* no. 10:52-56.

―――. 1971. "Musical instruments in Kiganda tradition and their place in the East African scene." *Essays on music and history in Africa.*:93-135.

Wachsmann, Klaus P. Kay Russell. 1971. "The Interrelations of Musical Instruments, Musical Forms, and Cultural Systems in Africa." *Technology and Culture* 12 (3):399-413.

Westermann, Diedrich Bryan M. A. Arnott D. W. 1970. *The languages of West Africa.* Folkestone; London: Dawsons.

Wiggins, Trevor & Kobom Joseph. 1992. *Xylophone music from Ghana.* Crown Point, IN: White Cliffs Media Co.

Wilson, Godfrey. 1939. *Nyakyusa conventions of burial.* Johannesburg: University of the Witwatersrand Press.

In der Reihe „Center for World Music – Studies in Music"
(ISSN 2367-4547) erschienen bisher folgende Titel:

Band 1
Lisa Gaupp: Die exotisierte
Stadt. Kulturpolitik und
Musikvermittlung im
postmigrantischen Prozess
Hildesheim: Universitätsverlag;
Hildesheim, Zürich, New York:
Georg Olms Verlag, 2016. – 458 S.
ISBN 987-3-487-15423-7

Band 2
Keivan Aghamohseni: Tango
auf dem persischen Teppich.
Das Medium Schellackplatte im
Kontext von Modernisierung
und Nationalismus im Iran
Hildesheim: Universitätsverlag;
Hildesheim, Zürich, New York:
Georg Olms Verlag, 2017. – 291 S.
ISBN 978-3-487-15548-7

Band 3
Barbara Alge:
Forschungsdatenmanagement
in der Musikethnologie
Hildesheim: Universitätsverlag;
Hildesheim, Zürich, New York:
Georg Olms Verlag, 2019. – 107 S.
978-3-487-15835-8

Band 4
Nepomuk Riva: Wissenschaft unter
Beschuss / Academia under Attack
Hildesheim: Universitätsverlag;
Hildesheim, Zürich, New York:
Georg Olms Verlag, 2020. – 328 S.
978-3-487-15862-4